THINKING
OUT HOW
THE

THINKING
OUT
THE HOW

TED KOLDERIE

CENTER
FOR POLICY
DESIGN PRESS

ISBN 13: 978-1-7362007-3-5

Cover and interior design by James Monroe Design, LLC.

Center for Policy Design Press
332 Minnesota Street W1360
St. Paul, Minnesota 55101
www.centerforpolicy.org

To talk long beforehand of things to be done, is unpleasant . . . but I do not mean by this to discourage you from proposing any plans which you may conceive to be beneficial, after having weighed them well in your own mind; on the contrary, I request you to do it with the utmost freedom, for the more combined and distant things are seen, the more likely they are to be turned to advantage.

—GEORGE WASHINGTON, 1797

CONTENTS

EVENTS

Policy Action

Data

Public Debate

Values

Proposal-Development
Problem-Analysis
Issue-Clarification

"Issues"
Discussion

Problem-Identification

INTRODUCTION:

THE IMPORTANCE OF
FINDING THE 'HOW'

I started out to write some recollections of public life in Minnesota ... and along the way came to see the more-than-historical dimension of what I'd been watching and had to some extent participated in. So this has become a book mainly about the process of policy-making, about the importance of the civic sector in generating ideas for people in politics—with particular attention to policy for public education.

Minnesota has been a successful state. A sound economy. Good politics. Strong institutions. With less than two per cent of the nation's population, a state playing a significant national role. A state more opportunity-driven than crisis-driven.

Our success comes in significant degree from having had a superior capacity to adapt, as the nation's economy and society have changed. That capacity, in turn, comes from our having had both sound governmental institutions and a strong civic sector.

Today, though, there is real concern. It is common to hear people say that politics—partisan, polarized and increasingly ideological—no longer works.

Though widely accepted, that criticism might be unfair. The problem might be the 'crumbling' of the civic infrastructure that for so long helped override the unattractive features of politics, including its difficulty in putting the public interest ahead of special interests.

It was our civic sector that did so much to shape and define the issues and to generate good ideas for those in public life to use. Today—and consider what you hear about public education—the policy discussion consists largely of deploring problems and reaffirming goals, as if 'being concerned' and 'being committed' by itself accomplishes something.

There has to be a 'how'

That sort of discussion lacks a 'how'. And there has to be a 'how' . . . some way by which the concerns can be dealt with and the goals achieved. Without a 'how' the promises made in politics will come up empty and the public, frustrated, will become cynical and turn against politics. With reason.

So we need to talk about the 'how'. Finding it requires us to examine our systems and institutions, to identify the incentives that cause the organizational problems and behaviors we dislike . . . and that at the same time make it difficult for people in public office to deal with those problems. We need to understand how to redesign our institutions so they work effectively, equitably, responsively, economically.

Institutional design is not the political sector's strength. Candidates for office campaign on problems and visions, leaving the 'how' for later. The winners need a strong civic sector to bring them proposals. This partnership worked when Minnesota was in its most successful years. Perhaps the recollections in this book will help explain that process, and what needs to be reestablished.

Of course Minnesota is different now. Of course the solutions applied before might not apply today. All I say is that after all the airing of problems, after all the discussion about 'who' and 'what' is responsible, after the protests and the promises to change and to do better, there is no success unless there is a 'how'—and a process for thinking out the 'how'.

As I finish this book . . . after 60 years around public life . . . I find myself as confident as I have ever been about anything that in our recent discussions here in Minnesota we are coming to see the 'how' . . . coming to see, for example, that for public education the successful strategy is 'innovation-based systemic reform', linked to teacher professionalism. And coming to see that, for a sound politics, 'liberal decentralism' is the simple, central idea for the difficult years ahead.

Bear with me as I try to explain.

SECTION ONE:

LEARNING

Looking back, my career in public affairs seems perfectly coherent. Everything I did laid a foundation for what came next; every stage followed logically out of the one before it. There were no false starts; no cul-de-sacs or reversals. It looks beautifully planned.

It was in fact anything but. No way was a career in public affairs predictable from the family context. No way did school or college point me this direction. Nor at the start did I see myself becoming an observer of public affairs—let alone a participant in them. Things simply happened. Opportunities presented themselves; I said yes or no, and largely with sheer luck moved along a path. After the Star and Tribune I never sought a job and never did a resume except to be introduced as a speaker or identified for something I'd written. You go along; life presents certain opportunities; you accept or not. Asked when coaching the Minnesota Vikings why he made some particular decision, Bud Grant would say: "It seemed like the right thing to do". It was like that.

Strangely, it worked out. I found that organizations and individuals can be influential working with ideas rather than with money or votes or the power of office. An outsider is free to think about and talk about what ought to be done; is not constrained by the insiders' notion that "Politics is the art of the possible". You look for those who believe that "Politics is the art of making possible what is necessary"; those who are open to the new understandings and ideas that drive change. Ideas matter: Read Theodore H. White's **In Search of History.**

Explaining what is necessary—and showing how it might be made possible—requires being close to the action yet not quite in it, moving between the big institutions of government and politics, working with the people who are trying to make things better; requires time to think and learn and especially the independence to say and to write what will discomfit current and conventional opinion.

I was lucky enough to be able to do that kind of civic work; first with the Star and Tribune, then with the Citizens League and later at the (then) Humphrey Institute—after which I became able financially to do this on my own.

Initially I would not have thought that possible. But we're now told that simply working at something long enough—"10,000 hours"—enables almost anyone to do something well. Perhaps that extends even to 'large-system architecture'. If so, then providing young people that opportunity must be important to the success of a community . . . as I hope the story told here will confirm.

It probably helped for my work to have made me a generalist, exposed to a variety of institutions and policy problems and having to understand and to explain how the various systems worked. Looking back I count: farm policy; river basin development (irrigation, navigation, flood control); area electric power supply; the oil industry; the media (newspapers, public radio and television); state/local electoral politics; state government organization and legislative process; local government organization and 'charter reform'; public finance and property taxation; Selective Service (the draft); hospital planning; child day care; the postal service (the 'delivery system'); and metropolitan issues (sewerage, water supply, solid waste disposal, housing and urban renewal, land use planning, freeway planning, transit development); regional governmental structure; nonprofit organization and philanthropy. As well as education policy and school finance.

To set the background I begin with growing up in Omaha in the 1930s and '40s. Chapter 2 tells the story of an English major drifting into public affairs, into the graduate school at Princeton, and describes my further education as a Pfc in the Army. Chapter 3 covers my 'post-graduate' work for the Minneapolis Tribune in North Dakota.

Somewhat better educated by then, I returned from North Dakota in 1959 to become the newspaper's City Hall reporter.

CHAPTER 1:

Omaha

My parents were an unusual pairing. My father, Ted, was the older son in a family that came from The Netherlands in 1912. His father had worked in the railway shops in Haarlem. I have the letter of recommendation he brought with him, saying his last hourly pay was 29 cents. The family went first to Iowa; then moved to Minneapolis. His father started making streetcar bodies here; his mother cleaned houses. My mother, Helen, was the middle child in a merchant family in the small-town aristocracy in Jackson in southern Minnesota. They met at Carleton College; he there partly because he was good in track and partly because someone at Westminster Church had noticed and liked his drive and lent him the money to go.

Years later I found a photo taken on their wedding day, in the house in Jackson. The mothers of the bride and groom in their very different dresses stand behind my mother's grandmothers, seated, dressed in their widows' black. I remember these ladies looking just like that on our visits to Jackson in later years: Alice Gillespie and Bessie Hunter, the latter still there when I was almost nine. I did the arithmetic: These ladies were teen-agers when Lincoln was president.

It was a then-typical middle-class bringing-up: Mother at home; Dad on the road, covering Nebraska for Josten's. Small schools; small towns where you could buy a steak dinner for 25 cents. With school out, summers were free and with prices low they traveled: driving to Los Angeles for the Olympics in '32; cruising down the St. Lawrence and through Alaska's inland passage. Omaha was a tough place to live. In 1934, the year my sister Kay was born, it was over 100 for 30 days in the summer, below zero for 30 days in the winter. I remember the dust storms; the Missouri river flooding. Soon, summers, the family went to northern Minnesota. Al Woock built my parents a cabin on Ten Mile lake in 1940.

The '30s were the Depression, but I'd known nothing else. I can see Mr. Dinsmore selling groceries from his truck. We played in the vacant lots. Stole clothesline. Biked everywhere. Went to Saturday matinees at the Dundee Theater for a nickel. Sat on Dodge Street counting the out-of-state license plates. The mailman came twice a day.

I read a lot. I borrowed from a lending library on Dodge Street: three cents a day, and I found the nice ladies didn't charge me if I brought the book back the same day. I read the World-Herald bellied-down on the living-room floor. I collected stamps.

My teachers at Dundee School didn't know much about anything except language. I had two years with Ella Egan diagramming sentences, from which I did learn grammar. I remember the 16mm ERPI films: "Bring the World to the Classroom". One image never left me: People in the jungle building a bridge by drawing one vine after another back and forth across the river.

I carried the old Saturday Evening Post; pushed doorbells, asked people to buy. "You never succeed taking 'no' for an answer", my salesman-father advised. I shoveled endless sidewalks and driveways for a dollar; Omaha's heavy wet snow that has to be lifted.

In May 1940 when the Germans went into Holland my father sent me to the corner to buy the World-Herald 'extra'. Later a letter came from an uncle there, smuggled out through Belgium, to be forwarded to the Dutch East Indies. It came back the following summer, opened by censors: The Japanese had gotten there first.

As 11-year-olds we stood outside the school the morning after, talking about Pearl Harbor. Gas rationing came: my father had a B sticker. I rolled my wagon around, collecting metal and bacon grease for the war effort: It was incredible what came out of basements. I followed the war pinning flags in maps. Our teacher said we had to stay after school if we did not buy war stamps. That seemed wrong. Jim Cornish had a hectograph machine and we denounced this in a pamphlet we titled "The Underground". It was my first venture into journalism. The teacher was furious. But I did notice the practice stopped.

In 1941 we moved to North 53rd street. I remember going down Military Avenue with Warren Buffett, collecting bottle caps. In 1944 I started at Benson High. The Bunnies. It was an innocent time. Everybody rode bikes; nobody stole bikes. Because our family went north when school was out I missed what others did through the summer. I did go to camp at White Earth, with Niels Thorpe, swimming coach at the University of Minnesota; learned to swim, sail a boat, shoot a rifle.

I was in ROTC; on the rifle team; regularly walked to school carrying my Winchester 52 and live ammunition. We were in cars all the time; riding around. The school always had us doing something. The Benson High News was one of the country's best high-school papers; my only vocational training. Project-based learning, we'd say today. Gunnar Horn ran the journalism program. One Monday in 1946 he came in, sat down, opened a copy of the New Yorker and began reading. For the whole period. Every day. For the whole week. It was John Hersey's **Hiroshima**.

In 1948 I graduated. It was automatic, almost, to go to Carleton. And in September I was off.

CHAPTER 2:

Three Educations

The concept of 'education' here might seem a bit awkward: college and graduate school and also the army, which for me certainly was an education. As was my initial work for the Star and Tribune, on the police beat and in North Dakota—which will get a separate chapter.

College: Carleton

In September 1948 when I arrived in Northfield the last class of veterans was beginning its senior year. The student body became again mostly the sons and daughters of business and professional people in the Midwest. It was not an activist campus. The college's famous graduate, Thorstein Veblen, was never mentioned. President Gould ran the place with a firm hand. Chapel was compulsory; the women wore hats. Hours were strict. No cars.

It was a traditional education; academic disciplines, unconnected (despite Gould's effort my freshman year). I wish we had been able to look at the literature, history, politics and science of, say, the 17th century all together. But I did absorb the concept of a liberal education.

Particularly Milton; truth emerging from the clash of ideas. Predictably, I had drifted into the English department: Professor Elledge, teaching with questions. But I found myself increasingly interested in American history. I asked about arranging an American Studies major. Authority frowned. Not approved.

I was pretty alone my sophomore year. The next fall new roommates took me in hand; Evan's friend arranged a first date for me with a sophomore I'd noticed: Midge Quick. We were engaged my senior year.

My last year it was decided that Willis Hall—Carleton's 'Old Main'— should become the (first) student union. That had been the dream of the longtime head of buildings and grounds. I suggested it would be better, more logical, for the union to go into the old gym when a new gym was built, as it was soon to be. That was not appreciated. Visit today and you will see the union in the old gym. A lesson.

Coming out of college I had no idea what to do. I said 'no' to the newspaper at Stevens Point, Wisconsin. I thought about graduate school. American Studies seemed too much literature and the arts; nothing to do with that but teach. "The life of the mind" did not appeal. Somehow I came across the catalog for the public-affairs program at Princeton. I applied; went up to Saint Paul to interview with an early alumnus, Bob Holt. I am astonished today that I got accepted, having never had a course in either political science or economics. Looking back, this was a huge break; one of those accidents that shape careers. I think I owe a lot to Bob Holt.

I had an enjoyable summer reporting for the Daily Republican Eagle at Red Wing; Midge staying on in Northfield. I did the required reading: Max Lerner's **Ideas Are Weapons**. Karl Popper: **The Open Society and Its Enemies** (with the Pericles quote on the making of policy: "Although only a few might originate a policy, all of us are able to judge it"). Also, influenced by Professor Qualey, Schumpeter.

Graduate School: Princeton

Early in September I picked up a brown Plymouth at the factory in Michigan and drove to New Jersey. I had wanted to get to Princeton a day early. And did. It was disorienting for an innocent middlewesterner. The town. The campus. The Graduate College with its Proctor Hall (the "Ivory Tower"). Why would they have windows without screens? My roommate was Leighton Van Nort, a sociologist from Penn; my introduction to 'the demographic transition' and to Taft conservatism—which he defended around the Graduate College through the liberal politics of the 1952 campaign.

Then in its fifth year, the Woodrow Wilson School was taking 12 students annually for the two-year graduate program. Only a few just out of college. Some American military; captain to lieutenant colonel. Two from the Israeli military. Murray Weidenbaum from the Bureau of the Budget. Some from other nations' diplomatic service. The director, Donald Wallace, an economist, had been in the wartime price-control program. We had three seminars a week. The assignment in one for the opening week was Charles and Mary Beard's two-volume **Rise of American Civilization**.

Much of it was over my head. But it was good for the school not to be a trade school; to aim for a general understanding of policies and institutions. I remember the assumption about control, about planning, as a 'good'. Dissents like those of Hayek and Popper were mentioned but not discussed. I remember 'Wallace's laws': All controls spread; all controls wear out. Also: "Your generation tends to forget that wages are basically set by the demand for labor". Professor Levy: "Professionalism is one of the great hopes"—a view I later came to question. Professor Graham, in Washington during the war finding a statue of Edmund Burke; on the base the quotation: "Magnanimity, in politics, is not seldom the truest virtue".

In the summer of '53 I found an internship with Dave Freeman at the Fund for the Republic, then just spun off from the Ford Foundation to work on civil liberties. I got $45 a week. Stayed with George Bent who was living in a friend's house in Princeton. We rode the commuter train into Manhattan. Midge and I married in August; rented the top floor of a house on Moore Street.

The policy project the second year was on the making of foreign policy: Joachim Schumacher and I drew the press corps. Kim had been in the German army; captured in Tunisia he spent the rest of the war on a farm in Iowa. I think now that we should have concentrated more than we did on on the change then underway in American policy toward the USSR. I am still amazed at the access we had, to people in Washington and New York. At the New York Times, James Reston and others. At CBS, Eric Sevareid; Edward R. Murrow, telling again about the question Harry Hopkins asked him: Who does Churchill see most after midnight? In his house on Woodley Road, Walter Lippmann telling us how, in the summer of 1940, public behavior in London had in fact not been so admirable; how the government asked, perhaps told, the newspapers to write about the courage of Londoners under the bombing. People live up to the expectations set for them, was his point.

That second year I began to be interested in cities. I took a seminar in urban sociology and John Sly's course on state and local government—much of which was listening to his stories about the New York Port Authority and the politics of state tax policy. As chair of its commission on tax policy Sly was a critic of New Jersey's failure to have either an income or sales tax (which, later, I came to see as an way for New Jersey and Connecticut to rip off New York City). But I remember developing an understanding of federalism as the only practical response in a time when travel and communication made central control not-possible. I have thought about this more as travel and communication have become so rapid.

I audited Eric Goldman, then just finished writing **Rendezvous With Destiny**, his history of American reform. That gave me my first awareness of Herbert Croly selling to Theodore Roosevelt his idea of using the Hamiltonian state for Jeffersonian ends. I had a growing interest in the change in idea-systems. I realized I was beginning to collect books on the transition from laissez-faire to 'control' in the Progressive period and New Deal. Around this time I began reading The Economist.

I finished in June 1954 with no particular skills but with a fair understanding of major ideas, trends, patterns—the expansion, nationalization, democratization, industrialization, socialization of America. Seeing the fundamentals, patterns, the relationships among things, was beginning to seem important. I passed the general exam, which not all did.

So much had happened in two years. In 18 months, 15 trips across the Pennsylvania turnpike; reading books aloud in the car: Sevareid's **Not So Wild a Dream**; others. The question was: What next? Washington was not attractive. I passed on Arthur Adams' invitation to work at the American Council on Education. I thought about urban work; went to a meeting of redevelopment directors in Baltimore. I got an offer to work for the Housing and Home Finance Agency in Chicago. That didn't feel right. I interviewed with recruiters who came to talk with undergraduates; one afternoon, with Mr. Ross from Chase Bank. He worked with banks mainly in the Middle West; understood its appeal. Agreed: It has to feel right. He did say of banking: "It is one of the last businesses in which it is still possible to make great deal of money." I met with someone who came from NBC to talk about its management training program. To my astonishment, I was asked to New York to interview. To my greater astonishment I was invited into that program.

In Minneapolis earlier that year I had visited the Star and Tribune. I phoned Paul Swensson. He said I could have the next job open. So I went to New York and told NBC it didn't feel right. I didn't much like the East. Midge and I packed up the Plymouth; drove west without waiting for commencement to pick up my diploma. In the car that afternoon we listened to the Army/McCarthy hearings; Joe Welch zinging Senator McCarthy at last. It felt good to head west. Back to the land of the five-cent ice cream cone. Having left no real impression on anyone.

The Army

We lived in my uncle Adrian's house that summer, waiting for the Tribune job to open. I got an internship with the Citizens League.

Watched the Minneapolis City Council still in its 26-member chamber. Listened to a budget hearing; the fire chief in the red-painted Bank of England armchair, the "Hot Seat". Clearly there was much I did not know. A minor radio station gave the League a small program. We interviewed officials; did one with Alderman Frank Moulton and got his view of the city's role as "limited services and local housekeeping". I still have that LP record.

Then I was reclassified for the draft. I decided to volunteer; get it over. In November I went to basic training in El Paso. Arrived in a sandstorm. We lived in six-man 'huts'. There was hut discipline: If everyone behaved, all six could go out for the weekend. If anyone screwed up, nobody got out. In town an Italian family served a chicken cacciatore in their home for $1.65. Nobody screwed up. A lesson.

I was in Troop Information and Education; got assigned to the transportation center at Fort Eustis, Virginia—where I had my first exposure to railfans. We lived off-post: incredibly stumbled onto Mrs. Peachey's mansion in Williamsburg, its sun porch now an efficiency unit just being vacated by the executive director of Phi Beta Kappa who had finally persuaded the organization to move to Washington.

Seeing the huge organization as a Pfc was an experience. I came to appreciate Chester Barnard's perception that authority resides in the party *to whom* an order is given: You could tell that second lieutenants knew this. I came to admire the career RA cadre. One afternoon at Fort Eustis I was trying to interpret the ARs and SRs literally. Sfc Jones saw I needed help. "Ted", he said, "*Regulations*"—and he spread his hands wide—"*is a guide.*" To a significant degree it was the enlisted men who made the rule-based organization go; even the draftees with serial numbers beginning US sometimes had considerable influence. Our testing program turned up a man who'd finished 10th grade in Stamford, Connecticut but could not read. He was smart enough: Kindly people had been reading him the questions and writing down his answers. Suddenly there was no one to do that. I was advised to take the matter to Corporal Punsky in personnel. "Corporal Punsky is in conference", his assistant said.

I worked a transfer to Washington; to Walter Reed Hospital. But in September I was levied for Fort Churchill, Canada, on the west shore of Hudson's Bay; the Army's cold-dry test center. Midge and I hated the separation. While she worked I killed a few days wandering through the National Gallery; then took the long train ride out, through Winnipeg, across the muskeg to Churchill and to the post. Arrived, I went down to the shore and threw rocks in the water until the evening got too cold.

One evening Midge was on the radio from Washington; a signal through Resolute Bay. I looked at the map: Resolute Bay is as far north of Churchill as Churchill is north of Nebraska. I got out on leave to Washington. When I couldn't get the MATS flight back, we decided Midge would move to Saint Paul to wait out my tour.

Churchill was an experience: Four hundred miles beyond the end of the road; 50 below zero with 50-mph winds packing the snow so hard you could run across it in boots and hardly leave a mark. Discipline, not surprisingly, was lax. Tex, the company clerk, wondered what would happen if he requisitioned 10,000 sick slips. He got sent 10,000 sick slips.

We were in six-man rooms. Five college boys and one who hadn't finished high school, off the streets in Detroit, who'd chosen the Army as the alternative to prison after getting caught stealing from boats in the harbor; a federal offense. Very smart; very skillful; very loyal to his friends. I gave him my copy of **Why Did They Kill?** about a nurse beaten to death on the street in Detroit. Not far from where Bill had lived. He read it; a sociologist's interpretation. A few nights later flipped it back on my bed. "Crock of shit", he said. "Let me tell you how it really happens." And he did. Better than college.

One morning the First Sergeant caught us all sleeping in; ordered us down to Captain Botdorf's office immediately. Most of us would have confessed our guilt. Bill said: "Sir, the room leader did not wake us." The captain's face got redder as, knowing the rules, he struggled to decide whether to punish only the room leader. Finally he exploded: "Get out of here!" I always thought Bill could have been a successful lawyer or investigative reporter for a newspaper. But the last I knew he'd discovered railroad retirement and was headed for that system.

It was the International Geophysical Year; shooting Aerobee rockets into the ring of aurora that lies over Churchill; curtains of light directly overhead, the reds and greens and yellows playing back and forth horizon to horizon. Spectacular. At Christmas Midge flew up on a Canadian Pacific DC-3. Two friends built an igloo and the four of us had a memorable Christmas Eve.

I taught English grammar to the guys in the motor pool; found it challenging to explain why grammar mattered; the tools of the trade. You can't fix a truck with only a hammer and a screwdriver. I got some sense for "the people who live in the north". In the summer a few of us did a weekend up the Churchill River. Two old trappers taught us, I thought, something about the tradition in this part of the country. If crossing the forest you came to a cabin, someone might need help. You *had to* stop.

Discharged in September '56, I headed for Minneapolis.

CHAPTER 3 :

Reporting for the Tribune

At the Tribune they wanted me to start right away. I said I'd been away from Midge for a year and needed a week. So we had a beautiful seven days in the color in the woods at Ten Mile.

My first day the city editor, Danny Upham, had me come in early. As the reporters arrived and sat down, he told me who each was, what each did. Then he said: "You can divide them all into two groups. Some think they can do only what they've been told they can do. The others think they can do anything they haven't been told they can't do." Then he said: Here's where you sit.

I started on the police beat; 4 p.m. to 1 a.m. Accidents, fires, shootings; the police department and its culture. I remember Captain McClaskey: "Give me a good working stiff rather than a college boy any time".

Six months later I got the North Dakota assignment.

North Dakota

The Tribune had started keeping a reporter there about 1953. I was the third. In those days the Tribune gave home delivery almost to the Montana border. North Dakota was part of the 'hinterland' for which Minneapolis/Saint Paul was the regional capital for trade, transportation, finance. Frank Wright drove me around the state, getting acquainted—a rare example of training in the newspaper business. Then we settled at 931 Ninth Street in Bismarck, where a year later our son Paul was born.

I developed considerable respect for North Dakota; a much-misunderstood state. I'd had no appreciation for the Great Plains. "Nowhere else in the developed world", I later heard the geographer John Borchert say, "are so few people so highly organized to use so much land." On a train across Nebraska a woman put down her book; said, "Such endless monotony". Her seatmate, an older gentleman who had grown up on the plains, said: "It has always interested me why people from the East invariably think grandeur can only be vertical."

The assignment was a great education for me. Small scale; a state with only 13 urban places and fewer people than Hennepin County. Because everyone was needed it developed a high level of social competence. Frank drove me almost to Canada to meet Ralph Dewing, the Senate minority leader. A survivor of the USS Indianapolis. He was working in a restaurant, as I recall. On the floor of the Senate, when the Republican majority leader was struggling with procedure, Ralph would help him out. He later was director of management and budget for the state.

It was the scene of the last farmers' revolt, 1916-17; their Nonpartisan League (NPL) taking control of the majority party, a lesson in the 'how' of political power. They created a state bank to leverage on the Minneapolis banks and a state mill and elevator to leverage on the grain trade. The proposal from their superintendent of public instruction to the 1919 legislature is a classic, insisting on—and explaining how to get—an equitable education for "the rural child", only a third of whom were then finishing the eighth grade.

Many active then were still around. I remember a woman in Dickinson. "It was a wonderful thing to have lived through it", she said. "It was a crusade. Now"—and she waved her hand toward her television set—"nothing". A.C. Townley, the organizer of the NPL, could still be found, evenings, in some hotel. Later I was the only outsider at his funeral.

The Missouri Basin development program was under way. In a hotel room in Pierre I asked a man with the rivers-and-harbors interests about the conflict over appropriations for navigation, irrigation, recreation, flood control. "Son", he said, "I'm a lobbyist. We don't fight over shares. We work for a bigger pie." I thought Bruce Johnson, in charge of the Garrison Diversion project for the Department of the Interior, a fine type of federal civil servant. He'd come from a small town near Dickinson. He remembered his father opposed when everyone else was advocating a hard-surface road to Dickinson. "That will kill our town", his father said. Everyone wanted the road. It did kill their town.

I was on my own in this job; essentially a foreign correspondent in a state wanting not to be a colony of the Twin Cities. Being covered by the Minneapolis newspaper was important. Occasionally there was a short wait to see the governor. I covered the farm programs. (Early, I learned never, on the plains, to complain about rain.) For Sunday's paper I wired an oil column, which the Tribune carried for investors in Minneapolis. I started writing for The Economist, John Midgely then its Washington correspondent.

Basically the job was to write the best story in the state every day. There was the tornado at Fargo, the prison riot at Bismarck, human-interest stories. I learned how you fight a prairie fire. Don't get in front of it. Get sprayers at both ends; walk along with it as it moves, narrowing it gradually. (There might be a lesson here, too.)

The 1959 session was my first look at a state legislature. North Dakota's met for 60 days every two years; heard every bill in committee, voted on every bill on the floor and got done on time. The Legislative Research Committee (LRC) worked through the major issues in the 'off' year; had bills ready when the session convened.

At the end of the '59 session the dairy interests in Cass County tried to restrict Minnesota milk coming into North Dakota. When the bill passed the Senate most newspapers warned a serious problem was looming for consumers. A friend on the LRC staff told me the senators' vote was a favor to their colleague from Cass County, about to retire. So the Minneapolis Tribune reported the bill had passed the Senate and been sent to the House "where it will be killed". As it was.

A couple of weeks later I turned everything over to Mercer Cross. We drove to Minneapolis and moved into a double-bungalow on E. 46th St.

Back to Minneapolis

The Tribune in 1959 was basically still a new paper; the old morning paper given new life when Dayton's began to advertise on Sunday. Daryle Feldmeir had gone almost directly from reporter to managing editor. Sam Romer, covering labor, had grown up in Detroit, been an organizer for the Garment Workers, gone to Spain, been a labor adviser to the American occupation in Japan. Dan Hafrey, covering welfare and religion, had gotten out of Latvia through Russia just before the German invasion; went back to Europe with the American Army. Dick Kleeman covered education; John McDonald, politics; Victor Cohn, health and medicine. Across the newsroom sat the staff of the afternoon Star, some still at jobs they'd been doing for 20 years.

The Cowles had come to Minneapolis from Des Moines in the 1930s; gradually assembling the ownerships and renaming our region (carefully excluding Iowa) the "Upper Midwest". The Star and Tribune (as the company became) was by conviction internationalist in a state with an isolationist tradition. John Sr. was prominent in the Willkie campaign in 1940. Politics had revived in Minnesota with Stassen in the late '30s and, after the war, with Luther Youngdahl. Civic life revived in Minneapolis with Hubert Humphrey. The newspaper was deeply involved: in the clean-up of the Minneapolis police department, with Humphrey's effort to end discrimination (initially, Minneapolis' anti-Semitism) and in the '50s with the rebuilding of the city.

It takes an effort today to visualize what Minneapolis—Minnesota, this country—was like into the 1950s. Most everything was smaller-scale. News was more local. America was not even a single country. In the South the post-Reconstruction politics and racial segregation still prevailed. Every major-league baseball team was north and east of St. Louis. The Interstate Highway system was still in planning. No airplane had yet flown nonstop coast to coast.

Minneapolis treated Saint Paul as a rival; as a different, distant place. I remember, visiting my grandparents in the late 1930s, looking across the Lake Street bridge at the ornamental lighting along East River Road, wondering what was over there. The two were still very much independent cities. Not surprisingly: This was a unique form of twin cities; the two downtowns not on opposite ends of a bridge across the river but 15 miles apart along the Mississippi. Minneapolis and Saint Paul grew together at their residential edges.

The newspaper as an educational institution

In the community and in its civic life the Star and Tribune—as a newspaper and as a business—was vastly more important than it is today. When dedicating the new/remodeled building in 1949, John Sr. observed that from the time they left school (and in 1950 most adults in Minnesota had barely been to high school) most people got most of their information from newspapers. While his paper would cover national and world affairs the primary obligation of the Star and Tribune, he said, was to provide information about its region. The newspaper should take seriously its obligation as an educational institution. He wanted its reporters to think of themselves as the equivalent of a college professor. You heard about that when you joined the Star and Tribune in those years, not from management but from the other reporters.

The beat reporters were not oriented to 'the general reader'. We wanted to tell people on our beat things they did not know were happening in their field. And often we could. I wrote the oil column from Bismarck every Friday night, I know, to tell scouts things they could not learn directly about developments in competing companies, or about discussions in the Industrial Commission that regulated the industry and allocated the monthly production quotas. Anticipating the discovery of oil, North Dakota had put a regulatory framework in place before Amerada brought in the Matt Iverson #1. The night before a commission meeting, downtown at the GP Hotel, Doc Laird and Bert Folsom could be found after dinner (Bert drinking grasshoppers; horrible things), talking about what was coming up the next day. After the commission meeting the members retreated to the governor's office to talk about what to decide and do. They weren't enthusiastic about my sitting in with them, but neither did they throw me out when I sometimes did.

Reporters wanted to know, were expected to know, as much as possible about what was going on; what was happening and why it was happening. George Thiss, Republican state chairman, said that when Frank Wright called, "I knew I was going to get asked the question I least wanted to answer that day". The 'why' was important. Frank Premack while city editor became famous (or notorious) for asking reporters to explain 'why'. We did not write all we knew: The ethic in those days carried some responsibility for the process. Sam Romer told the desk he'd write the full story when the strike was over. Trust mattered. Public officials found it in their interest to have reporters informed; knowledgeable about the way things worked. So it was a learning experience; on-the-job training. Only the newspapers did this. Real journalists had little time for the 'news readers' in radio and television.

Reporters were still willing to be critical. One state senator ran a particularly scruffy nursing home in Minneapolis. Jack McDonald, the state government reporter, regularly wrote about the place and the criticisms of it by inspectors. "McDonald, when are you going to write something good about me?", the senator asked him once. "When am I going to *hear* something good about you?" Jack replied.

Generally, the close relationship prevailed; the writing for 'insiders' that in later years would come to be put down by new-era journalists. Newspaper people and public officials mingled socially. The Premack living room was famous for this. When Frank died of a heart attack in 1975 there was the usual journalist secular service. The publisher and top editors of the Star and Tribune came; the governor and the attorney general and the chairs of the two political parties came.

That the Star and Tribune was not universally liked became evident in 1962 when the Teamsters' strike shut the papers for about four months. The Guild, the reporters, went out in support. The Daily American appeared. That shook the Cowles, happening just as John Sr. was turning the paper over to his son. Soon after publication resumed, John Jr. fired Bill Elston, the editor of the editorial page where I was then working. I stopped by Bill's house on my way home that Saturday morning to tell him this rumor was around the newsroom. "It's true", he said. We went downstairs and he explained; how he'd told the ownership how removed it was from what reporters and editorial writers had always known and had to face every day.

In the mid-1960s the Star and Tribune began letting the beat reporters follow their stories into the legislative process. The Capitol reporters had covered everything as a political story: who's up and who's down; the tax bill the only story of substance. When the Legislature's actions on education, welfare, labor, business and metropolitan government began to be covered by reporters who knew those fields, the policy process changed. Things possible before were now not possible. Things that had not been possible became possible because of the attention the reporting gave to the proposals for change and to their authors.

It was a great learning experience; an endless education. I remember Dave Mazie saying at one point: "There's never been a day I came to work that I couldn't count on something new and interesting happening." Not everyone is so lucky.

This was the setting into which I was dropped as I became City Hall reporter for the Tribune in the spring of 1959. The physical re-construction of Minneapolis was just beginning. A redevelopment authority had been created in 1947; federal financing had come in 1954. The Interstate Highway program had been enacted in 1956; our freeways were just being designed. So the push was on for city planning in Minneapolis and Saint Paul—just as the Twin Cities area was outgrowing the two central cities. All this was about to produce a torrent of change.

I had been reading up on Minneapolis while in North Dakota, getting ready for the City Hall beat. Pending my arrival the desk had put Ed Magnuson into City Hall, over his objections. He found he liked it; wanted to stay. But they kept their promise to me. Soon after, Ed went to TIME where over the years, I was later told, he wrote more cover stories than anyone who ever worked for the magazine.

With the job in City Hall I started, unknowingly, a career not really in journalism but in public affairs.

SECTION TWO:

INSTITUTIONS FOR A NEW 'CITY'

It was a good time to come into public life and the Star and Tribune was a good base to be working from. On the City Hall beat I watched people trying to do things. As I saw them running into difficulties I began to think about the problems and how they might be overcome. City Hall insiders insisted "It's the people who count". But I began to see that sometimes the system shaped the way the people behaved.

The assignment was to cover Minneapolis city government: urban redevelopment, roads and freeways, governmental organization, finance and operation. I describe these in Chapter 4. Quickly, though, 'the city' took on larger dimensions as after 1960 Minneapolis and Saint Paul became more and more entangled with the suburbs around them. Chapter 5 describes how

Minnesota went about reconstructing local government in the Twin Cities region.

The Star and Tribune—and its editorial pages, to which I moved in 1961—provided a superior access to public affairs, the time and the opportunity to think and to generate proposals. And of course the medium of the state's largest newspaper.

Chapter 6 describes another such 'setting'—the Citizens League—to which I went, as executive director, in the summer of 1967. It had become a remarkable civic mechanism for considering "what are the problems and opportunities of this community, and what could and should be done about them". Chapter 7 relates the League's work in the 1960s and 1970s on the design of metropolitan arrangements, and especially with the difficult policy issues with roads and transit.

At this point in the book it will be clear that a strictly chronological approach does not work: The periods overlap; the next beginning while the current one phases down. The work on urban affairs ran into the 1970s. But in the '60s questions had begun to arise about public finance. So Section Three will turn back to recap those.

First, however: urban problems in Minneapolis.

CHAPTER 4:

Change Comes to Minneapolis

Minneapolis in the 1950s was just over 100 years old. Quickly after 1945 the four corners of the city were filled with ramblers. By 1960 it was almost fully developed. What was later commonly said—that after the war people 'fled' the central city—was unfair; too simple. During the war people had doubled-up; in 1950 Minneapolis' population exceeded 520,000. The city was simply full. As the 'baby boom' began there was no place in the city for new families to live. They had to go to the suburbs.

Minneapolis in those years was basically sound. The 1954 interview with Frank Moulton came back to me: the City Council's job as limited services and local housekeeping. Plat the subdivisions, provide fire and police service; collect the garbage, build some arterial streets, maintain the residential streets (many still oiled-dirt).

This was the role for which the city government was structured: an English borough form; institutionally weak, an exoskeleton supported by a strong civic culture on the outside. As in the English model it was a strong-council system, with a mayor in a minor role (appointing only the chief of police and serving on various boards and commissions) and with no strong central administration. Departments other than police reported to committees of the council; decisions were made there, then ratified by the council in full session. The council majority chose a leader. Moulton, the 10th ward alderman, dominated the majority group; in the famous distinction 'a politician of non-movement'. In the 1930s Minneapolis had borrowed heavily to pay relief. When elected, Frank led the debt-reduction policy. His idea of good government was to hold down spending—even in the early '50s when for a time the interest rate on municipal bonds was at or below one per cent.

In Minnesota the concentration of economic power in the Twin Cities was balanced by the political power of the rural area; its largest industry, agriculture, owned in thousands of small pieces all across the state. Until the 1970s this farmer politics dominated the state's government. The deal was for the state to provide a basic level of services statewide and for Minneapolis and Saint Paul to pay, themselves, for the higher level of urban services they needed or wanted. So the cities had their own public hospitals, their own correctional institutions (workhouse and juvenile center). State aid paid for two lanes of a county road; if a wider road were needed the other lanes were paid-for locally.

As new and larger problems appeared, the state began to legislate. To clean up the Mississippi in the 1930s the state created a Minneapolis-Saint Paul Sanitary District: three members from each city and a chairman named by the governor. When the growth of airline service required a real airport the state created the Metropolitan Airports Commission, using the same system of representation.

All this was about to change. More complex problems were approaching.

Redevelopment in the central city

Victor Fischer taught me to see urban development in terms of two pebbles dropped in a pool: the first sending a ring of development out over open land; the second, dropped 100 years later, sending a ripple of *re*-development over the houses, streets and commercial structures built before. By 1950 the new development was moving out over farms in the second-tier suburbs; the re-development was moving from the old central core out over the city's older neighborhoods.

City planning was seen as a good thing and the Star and Tribune supported it both as a newspaper and as a company. It had been resisted by the City Council, which at one point got its attorney to reduce the planning commission's role to "statuary and other works of art". Planners desperately wanted influence. Minneapolis not having a powerful mayor, this initially meant going outside, for civic and business support. (In time they went to work for the City Council; giving up their independent role in return for influence over the Council's development program.)

The Twin Cities area was in those years an importer of urban know-how. It was fairly common for city officials and business people to talk together. They sometimes flew to other cities to see developments, sometimes on the Star and Tribune plane. Paul Veblen, an 'executive assistant in the newsroom', sat in meetings not open to reporters. He wrote memos to management about the issues in major development; distilled these into a Sunday 'Civic Progress' column. Occasionally a copy filtered down to the City Hall reporter. I noticed the librarian's name on the circulation list and found that back in the library, evenings, I could read the notebook in which he kept them. This was useful.

Urban renewal ran through the Housing and Redevelopment Authority (HRA); formally a state agency 'in and for the city of Minneapolis'. The redevelopment began on the old north side; the Glenwood project. But the old downtown was the major interest of the city and of the civic and business community. Its main street, Washington Avenue, was in truth not a 'skid row' but a community of elderly men who'd come here in the early 1900s to cut timber and harvest wheat. It got its bad reputation from the bars catering to visitors looking for drink and a good time.

After the Lower Loop project the idea was to re-do the residential neighborhoods. Bob Jorvig was by this time heading the redevelopment authority. The Tribune supported the HRA against Eddie Straus and his opposition to renewal, as it supported Larry Irvin and the planning department in its continual conflict with the City Council. Gradually, accommodating to the politics of the neighborhoods, clearance gave way to rehabilitation. Federal grants for renewal disappeared, replaced by tax-increment financing. That 'second ripple' of re-development continues; today can be seen down to Lake Street and up to Lowry Avenue.

At that time those displaced by redevelopment and by freeways were compensated for their property but had to bear themselves the costs of relocating their business. That seemed not right. I think I wrote an editorial after joining the opinion pages in the fall of 1961. I also went to see Bob Latz, the state senator representing north Minneapolis. Bob was able, fairly easily I believe, to get reasonable relocation expenditures made an element of the total project cost.

The freeways arrive

Two Interstate freeways were planned to cross at the Twin Cities: I-94, the east/west route from Chicago to Seattle and I-35, the north/south route from Dallas to Duluth. Politically, I-35 was split so there would be routes through both central Minneapolis and central Saint Paul. There would also be the usual circumferential.

Minneapolis' own planning had contemplated expressways diagonally out from downtown: It would have had to adapt to the north-south/east-west layout for the Interstates except that the System 5 computer runs showed a need for both. The Highway Department was unable to get approval for either the southwest or southeast diagonal, with the result that I-35W had to take all the traffic through south Minneapolis.

I recall Frank Marzitelli, the assistant commissioner of highways, one day telling a Minneapolis committee about a meeting with Archbishop Brady, the two of them down on their knees looking at the layouts and the archbishop saying, "You can have the national parishes, but leave my churches alone". His letter to Marzitelli recapping their understanding about the location of interchanges on I-94 in Saint Paul is a classic in urban transportation planning.

Because decisions in the developed cities were slow, easier in the suburbs, the freeway system was built from the outside in; the timing encouraging firms to locate in the suburbs as an alternative to their residents having to fight their way downtown. With the completion of the inter-city freeway Minneapolis' downtown gradually became the business, professional and retail center of the region, largely at the expense of downtown Saint Paul—demonstrating again that improving travel between two centers works to the advantage of the previously dominant center.

The decision-making arrangements were inadequate. The state needed decisions at two levels: on the regional system and on specific projects. For the system decision no municipality was large enough. For the project decisions the city was too large. So the system decisions on route locations and interchange design emerged from a complicated negotiation among the Highway Department, the city and the neighborhood; affected residents and owners insisting the neighborhood had a right to consent—while retaining, of course, their option to move away later.

Charter reform

The visible difficulty in decision-making lent importance to the old question of getting Minneapolis a more effective city government structure.

For years Minneapolis was governed by the collection of state laws applying to the city. After the home rule legislation early in the century several efforts to secure a new charter failed, and in 1920 the citizens simply adopted existing state law as a charter in the hope that over time it would be possible by amendment to get something better. Such an effort was organized during Humphrey's time as mayor. A strong-mayor system on the model then appearing in cities in the East was on its way to a vote in the fall of 1948. It failed when Humphrey pulled out to run for the Senate. The Citizens League was formed in 1952 largely to carry on this work.

In the mid-1950s a minor change, perhaps a reprisal for the council's opposition in 1948, reduced the number of aldermen from 26 to 13.

After Verne Johnson arrived in 1958 to be executive director, the Citizens League led another effort for the strong-mayor system in 1960. The charter commission, created to be a planning commission for government structure, was captive to the council, whose members tended to feel that questions about the structure of government belong to the people who work in it. So the League bypassed the commission; went the petition route with the CIVIC Charter campaign. "Dictator charter", City Hall responded. The effort failed by an even larger margin than before. I covered this campaign, objectively. I think the League was disappointed.

The debate taught me several lessons about change and 'reform'. Proponents of change attack the visible evils of the present and talk about how well things will work after their reform is adopted. Defenders of the existing order tell you how well things work *in theory*, and what terrible things would result were change to be introduced; "spreading fear and doubt", as Verne said. (I thought there was a lesson in the existing charter's provision about redistricting. The charter provided that should the Council fail to redistrict, the job would automatically go to the three persons the alderman disliked most: the mayor, the comptroller and the president of the Board of Estimate. The Council always did the redistricting on time.)

Spending most of every day in City Hall, I developed a considerable respect for the people in city government; for a good alderman's ability almost to see every street corner in the ward. I came to appreciate their sense that 'reform' implied something criminal: reform school; reformatory. (Years later, in a dinner discussion, Martin Sabo leaned over and whispered, "I *hate* the term 'reform'.")

Two efforts to "shoot the moon", to replace Minneapolis' strong-council form with a strong-mayor form, had now failed. There would be one more such effort before thinking turned another direction.

In Saint Paul the same questions about governmental structure were being worked-through. None of that was on my beat: The Tribune covered Saint Paul with Paul Presbrey, basically as a police story. There was little downtown redevelopment. Freeway location seemed easier: Saint Paul had relationships with the Highway Department that Minneapolis envied. When Saint Paul's charter commission asked voters to swap the city's commission form for a strong-mayor form they said 'yes' almost immediately.

New growth beyond the city; 'sub-urban' issues

As people moved into the suburbs the newspapers had to change. Reporters accustomed to writing that Elmer Johnson lived in 'Minneapolis' now had to look up the municipality; write that he lived in, say, Plymouth or New Hope. More important, the central city began to be caught up in issues with the suburbs and decisions became inter-governmental.

I began writing about these disputes off the City Hall beat; found myself increasingly at night meetings in the suburbs. But the Star was to be the local paper, covering the nighttime suburban council meetings. In 1960 management asked me to go over to the Star side as assistant city editor to help handle the suburban coverage. Newsroom wisdom being always to say yes to what management 'asked', I did that.

The suburbs had been improving as well as growing. Orville Peterson, with the League of Municipalities, had persuaded the Legislature to put into law a procedure by which suburban 'village' government could convert to a manager form. Part of the revision of the Village Code finally enacted in 1949, this got competent front-line local government into place just ahead of the wave of suburban development; a marvelous case of institutional redesign.

Minneapolis looked down on the suburbs. Alderman Moulton famously suggested they "kept their budgets on wrapping paper". The city's attitude was: We put in and paid for our facilities; you put in and pay for yours. There was growing conflict over water supply, sewage disposal and cost-sharing in the Hennepin County programs.

I did some useful things while on the Star desk. I got Al Woodruff, the veteran county reporter, to teach the new suburban reporters how to calculate a property tax. But on the whole it was not a success. An editor's job is to think about what's in the paper. I got too involved with what was in the story, which of course irritated the reporters. Wisely, it was suggested I might be better suited to the editorial page. Quickly I agreed, and in the summer of 1961 went back there to think mainly about the urban issues.

Immediately that felt right. At that time there was a single staff, 16 people, writing for both papers. Most were older; some had started before the Cowles came. The tradition was for the editorial page to react to the morning headlines; offer opinions on what had happened. Editorial writers spent the day in the office; went out to the newsroom to ask reporters for background. Those of us newer to the editorial page wanted to get out of the office ourselves, listen in at the meetings, get ahead of the issues, suggest what public decisions ought to be.

I found I could get into meetings reporters could not. What I learned went into signed pieces as well as editorials. No one having told me I couldn't, I began to write the memos about development earlier done by Veblen and Upham. After a time reporters began coming to the editorial page to ask for background. At one point the Tribune's managing editor came back to suggest to Bob Smith, our editor, that the editorial pages ought not to comment on what had not been in the news columns. I believe Bob told him to go cover the news.

In April 1962 the Teamsters struck the paper. The Guild was out until August, in support. Most of us found work in public agencies. I went first to the Metropolitan Planning Commission. The day 740 River Drive opened most of the staff rushed out to see it: Our first high-rise! Towers in a park! Corbusier! Then I moved to the planning section of the Highway Department: Deane Wenger and Don Carroll; their computer analysis showing the engineers what freeways were needed where.

In 1963 Arthur Naftalin, now mayor, cranked up the third campaign for a strong-mayor charter reform. I did a series laying out the case. But the effort failed again, by an even larger margin. Clearly some different approach to the problem of city government structure was needed. But no one seemed to know what that might be. So charter reform was laid aside.

The redesign of Hennepin County government

From the editorial page it was possible to watch a variety of efforts at the redesign of local institutions.

The 1960 census required a redistricting of the county board, four of the members having until then come from Minneapolis and one from 'rural Hennepin'. The Citizens League was concerned that the warfare between city and suburbs not be structured into the newly-reapportioned board; intervened to persuade the commissioners to create one district wholly in Minneapolis, one wholly in the suburbs and three equally overlapping the city/suburban boundary.

It was another lesson about effective institutional design: With a majority of commissioners representing a mixed city/suburban constituency, the board had an incentive to focus on county-wide questions. With its Republican majority persuaded by Verne also to keep Stanley Cowle its administrator, Hennepin began to develop as one of the outstanding county governments of America.

The League and the county officials worked with the rising group of young Republican legislators in the suburbs in the 1963 session to create a countywide court of municipal jurisdiction, to expand the Hennepin County Park Reserve District and to transfer Minneapolis General Hospital to the county.

General Hospital, run by the city to care for indigents, had become a serious expense for Minneapolis. And it was about to become obsolete as insurance offering free choice of hospital ended the dual system of care. A Minneapolis task force trying to see the way ahead for the city heard Jack Dumas, its administrator, say: "The city gets out". It was one of several city functions Minneapolis was to turn over to Hennepin County as the city's role declined. Later: the workhouse, the juvenile facility, the welfare board and in 2008 its library system.

The election-night model

In 1963 I'd gone to a summer seminar for newspaper people put on by the American Political Science Association. One of those who came to speak was Warren Miller from the Survey Research Center at the University of Michigan. He had demolished a notion long cherished by newspapers and politicians.

"There is no 'horse race' on election night", Miller said. "Nobody ever leads; nobody ever trails. When the polls close somebody has won. The question is: How quickly can you find out who that is?" (Mail-in ballots then obviously not being a significant factor.) In 1962 they'd constructed for ABC television a 100-precinct 'scale model' of the Michigan electorate and arranged to have precinct results called in directly, bypassing the evening's Associated Press (AP) count through the counties. Bingo! Early on election night the scale model had a far more complete picture of what was happening; ABC could say by its 10 p.m. newscasts that George Romney had been elected.

The Star and Tribune had a problem reporting election results because in Minnesota, too, the AP had to wait for precinct returns to be driven to the county court house. With its Minnesota Poll the Star and Tribune could do what had been done in Michigan. But the news editors were not interested. They still saw Harry Truman in 1948 holding up that Chicago Tribune with its headline—"Dewey Defeats Truman"— and remembered the gubernatorial race in Minnesota in 1962, decided by 91 votes months later following a recount.

Bob Smith decided the editorial page would do the sample. So in 1964 Bob Coursen at the Poll created a stratified random 100-precinct 'scale model' of Minnesota. Charles Backstrom, University of Minnesota political scientist, wrote the computer program, then on punch-cards. I set up calls from the 100 precincts. It was 4 p.m. on election day when Backstrom got the program debugged. But it worked.

In 1966 the editorial pages wanted to run the model again. Harold LeVander was challenging Karl Rolvaag for governor. Walter Mondale was up against Bob Forsythe for the Senate. And this time, in addition to wanting an early call on the winner, we wanted to analyze why Minnesota voted the way it did. So using census figures we described each precinct in the sample in terms of age, race, religion, occupation.

As early as 9:30 on election night we had results from about half the precincts in the model, pretty much across the state: LeVander 52 per cent, Rolvaag 48 per cent. Off and on through the evening the Tribune managing editor, Daryle Feldmeir, would stroll over. We'd say: LeVander 52, Rolvaag 48. Feldmeir would nod; go back to the newsroom.

In Minnesota at that time the central cities with their voting machines reported early; gave a statewide DFL candidate a big 'lead'. Through the night as returns came in from outstate the Republicans would usually 'gain'. Late returns from northern Minnesota would then raise the DFL vote again. So: What to believe?

At press time, about 1 a.m., the AP count showing candidates 'neck and neck', the Tribune hedged its final headline: "Governor Election Close".

Some time after 3 a.m. Backstrom and I walked out through the newsroom carrying his computer prints. By that time, with most returns in from the courthouses, the AP was reporting LeVander 52, Rolvaag 48. Too late: Next morning's Tribune was already on the trucks. I can still see the news executives looking at us as we passed, realizing they'd had the story right there all night long.

Next morning, though, Feldmeir said it was good they had ignored the model. Look at the AP returns on the Senate race: Your model is way off on the votes cast. It could have been way off, too, on who won. You were lucky. We can't trust the model.

Backstrom went back over the numbers; finally said: Either there's an incredible statistical freak in our sample or the AP has a major counting error in the race for Senate. There was nothing to do but wait.

Some weeks later I looked up to see Frank Wright, the Tribune's political reporter, in my office doorway with a funny smile on his face. He said he had just come from the canvassing board—to which the official count is reported. "AP double-counted seven counties in northwestern Minnesota."

That—plus the election-analysis it produced—got the model accepted in the newsroom. Frank Premack, the new city editor, particularly liked it and in 1972 used it on the precinct caucuses, the first step in the process of candidate-selection. Since there is no counting-process, no 'horse race' on caucus night, the model produced truly new information for those who follow politics.

It was lesson about change—and the resistance to it—right at home.

Metropolitan issues arise

In the spring of 1965 the city elections pulled the editorial page back to municipal issues. Traditionally, the Star and Tribune spent the year criticizing Frank Moulton's policies and then supported his re-election on grounds he was "a good man to have around". I argued he was *not* a good man to have around; said we should oppose his re-election. The editorial calling for "a progressive city council" might have been effective: Moulton lost to Jack Newton. Frank sued to overturn the result on grounds Newton had unfairly represented the issues. Essentially Frank was suing the Star and Tribune, Newton having relied on what the editorial page had written. I testified. In his ruling for Newton Judge Amdahl said it was not for the courts to settle political disputes, especially when an incumbent had declined to respond to the charges himself during the campaign.

By 1965 city issues were giving way to regional issues, which had been rising for some years; problems beyond the reach of any single municipality or county. People were talking about regional and metropolitan; about a broader definition of 'the city'. But how were these to be decided; even discussed? The Metropolitan Planning Commission had appeared in 1957. But it had no decision-making authority, no real constituency and a Rube Goldberg structure of representation. Who would approve and implement its plans?

When the 1965 session failed to act on any metropolitan problem, even to act on the sewerage crisis, the metropolitan question moved to center stage. Clearly we needed to find a whole new process for the policymaking in the region, for issue-raising and for issue-resolving.

In time Minnesota found answers; a 'how' that was different from the rest of the country. That's a story in itself, and requires going back a bit to pick up the discussion that began in the late 1950s about 'metropolitan'.

CHAPTER 5:

The Regional City

By the mid-1950s it was clear that the sub-urbanization around the country's large central cities was creating a larger urban region—a 'metropolis'—that did not match the existing governmental framework. Quickly the question became how to plan, develop, serve and govern these metropolitan regions.

In a set of lectures at the University of Michigan in March 1961 Luther Gulick considered the need for some kind of metropolitan government. He decided the existing local governments were "immortal" and would block any new regional structure. The only possibility, he concluded, was cooperation among the existing levels; local, state and national.

That seemed too pessimistic. Surely Minnesota at least could do better. No state had so high a proportion of its population and economic activity concentrated in a single urban region. Almost from the beginning the state's policy had been to put everything into Minneapolis and Saint Paul: the state capital, the prison, the (combined state and land-grant) university, the state fair; over time the headquarters of most all the business firms and nonprofits. This policy of concentrating resources in a single location gave Minnesota, with two per cent of the nation's population, a metropolitan area of significant national rank. It seemed clearly in the state's interest to protect so important a state asset.

The need to get beyond the municipal city

In the popular discussion the concept of 'the city' was muddled. Journalists and others would come here, sometimes never leave the downtown, go home and write about 'Minneapolis'. Flying east, looking down at Detroit, its central business district looked like a golf ball under a corner of the rug of that huge urban region.

More than two million people lived in our region: "the Twin Cities" or "the Minneapolis-Saint Paul area". Geographically, Minneapolis was a *central* central city. Saint Paul, off to the east, was in John Borchert's view "Minneapolis' largest and most interesting suburb". All around, development stretched out; the rest of the real city.

Nature and history had not endowed all parts of our region equally. To the north, low-value development on the Anoka sand plain; to the west and south, high-value homes in the rolling wooded country. As in most urban areas the poor were concentrated in the central areas of Minneapolis and Saint Paul.

The governmental pattern was at the same time too much and too little: seven counties; about 160 municipalities; more than 80 school districts; assorted townships and special districts, including one for mosquito control. The central city municipal boundaries were too small to encompass the problems and systems of regional scale and too large for decisions of neighborhood scale. In his work for the Committee for Economic Development Alan Campbell wanted to say what he had come to believe and say privately; that "The central city boundary is the least relevant boundary in the American governmental system". Except in the South—where city/county consolidation was becoming popular—even a single county was too small. In Minnesota the regional structure designed by the state in the 1930s for sewerage and in the 1940s for airports, providing representation only for Minneapolis and Saint Paul, by 1960 no way reflected what the region had become.

No one advocated the state government should itself run the region's affairs. State legislation would be required, though, to restructure the region's governmental organization. State action, taking a regional perspective, could dramatically change 'the urban problem'. Common wisdom had it, for example, that cities were poor. But that was true only of the municipal city: Clearly the metropolitan city was a center of wealth. So the 'urban fiscal problem' was a function of the current governmental organization in which the real city was divided against itself.

One early initial impulse was to consolidate the local units within a region. With help from the Ford Foundation this was tried in Cleveland and St. Louis. It failed badly in referenda. That led some, like Gulick, to conclude that nothing was possible. Others continued to believe some regional solution ought to be possible. That seemed plausible for our region; the Twin Cities area (then) lying entirely within the boundaries of this one state. But what action? And, how accomplished?

Through the '60s and into the '70s Minnesota's Legislature did rework the system of local government organization and finance in the Twin Cities metropolitan area, arriving at arguably the best and most innovative approach of any state. It was a process in which, along with local governmental leadership, both the newspapers and the Citizens League played a crucial part.

Searching for a successful 'how'

The Legislature had done several things that helped lay the groundwork for regional development and governance: in 1947 by creating the redevelopment agencies, equipping the central cities to clear and rebuild, and in 1949 with the legislation introducing competent management into the suburbs. In 1957 Senator Elmer Andersen got legislation creating the Metropolitan Planning Commission (MPC). In 1959 Joe Robbie got the Legislature to create the Minnesota Municipal Commission to assert the interest of the state and of the broader public in an orderly process of municipal annexation and incorporation.

Then suddenly in 1959 larger questions about regional operating systems were triggered by the groundwater contamination problem; after the woman in New Hope called the Health Department to say, "I took a glass of water out of my tap and it has a head on it like beer". Tens of thousands of households were putting their dishwater and sewage into, and drawing their drinking water from, the back yard.

The water-supply side of it was solved fairly quickly; the suburbs choosing either to drill deep wells or to buy water from Minneapolis or Saint Paul. Water can be pumped. But sewage is gravity-flow, and that required a larger-scale solution.

The central cities were prepared to sell treatment at their down-river plant. But the suburbs initially wanted their own plants. One sub-regional group proposed to discharge into the Mississippi north of Minneapolis, which seemed to violate the Boy Scout rule about not peeing upstream from the campsite. Another proposed to discharge into Lake Minnetonka. I remember a consultant holding up two vials of water: one cloudy, which came from the lake; another crystal-clear, which he said came out the pipe from a treatment plant. He didn't mention that the second was loaded with chemical nutrients.

In the 1959 session and again in 1961 the Legislature could not resolve the controversy. Frustrated, Senator Rosenmeier in 1963 put through a bill for a state solution; directing the commissioner of administration to design a system, build it, and levy the taxes. So strong a state action could not be implemented politically. So in 1965 the conflict returned. And again the Legislature could not act.

The Citizens League and others had been trying to think how to get a metropolitan policy body able to generate a solution. They looked at metropolitan efforts elsewhere; drawing on the Advisory Commission on Intergovernmental Relations (ACIR): Bill Colman, Norm Beckman, Dave Walker. We found mostly false starts. Locally, the Metropolitan Planning Commission was at work. Also the geographers on the Upper Midwest Urban Study. Mayors were actively in discussion. The Legislature had set up 'metro affairs' committees. All looking for the 'how'.

One idea getting attention was for a regional 'council of governments' (COG), with members representing the local cities and counties. This had been conceived by Kent Mathewson while city manager in Salem, Oregon. Thinking about it, the League people were skeptical; believed a collection of local officials would be ineffective as a mechanism for making serious regional decisions. Mathewson himself, we discovered—by now with the Metropolitan Fund in Detroit—had re-thought the COG idea and by '65 believed it inadequate.

I was part of this discussion, at the Star and Tribune. At the Dispatch/Pioneer Press in Saint Paul the executive editor, John Finnegan, had taken an interest in regional affairs; was serving on the MPC. When one of his reporters, Peter Vanderpoel, asked to pursue these metropolitan questions, Jack told him to go ahead.

It was coming clearer how to make the metropolitan perspective attractive politically. Major-league baseball and football had just come to the Twin Cities area, after years when Minneapolis and Saint Paul each had a minor-league team. Initially each city was wooing the New York Giants and the Washington Senators. Baseball saw our area as a single region; made it clear there would be one major league team here. That set the question. Separately, Minneapolis and Saint Paul could be the 27th and 43rd largest cities of America; minor-league. Or, if we would think of ourselves as a single regional city, we could be the 15th largest; major-league. Which would we rather be?

The logic was irresistible. It was a question, of course, whether logic would prevail.

In the fall of 1965 I wrote a series for the Star: "Our Metropolitan Future". It hit on the distinction between the municipal city and the real city. And tried to show the progress of the debate—including a proposal from state Rep. Douglas Head for a regional body with representation based on state legislative districts, members chosen by the legislators in those districts.

The national effort at a 'council of governments'

I had put in for a Congressional Fellowship; had been accepted, and just as that Star series appeared, went off to Washington. There, beginning in Fall 1965, I was able to watch how 'the urban problem' was being approached on the national level.

The group of fellows was half journalists and half assistant professors of political science. All were sure they wanted to work only for a member of the Democratic Study Group. A Republican? No way. A rural Republican? Impossible. I went to Al Quie, the congressman from rural southeastern Minnesota, and he agreed to meet. I got some of the fellows to come one afternoon to the old Union Station. Al folded his hands on the table; farmer's hands, bigger than they had ever seen. He gave them his big smile and began to talk with deep understanding about the House; its people, its procedures, its culture. That was the last I heard about 'rural Republicans'.

The House half of the fellowship I spent with Rep. Henry Reuss; his subcommittee on urban research. For a hearing on housing I interviewed the lobbyist for the brick industry, Douglas Whitlock; listened for two-hours, came back and wrote it all down.

At one point Henry said: "Get me a position on the draft". This led to another 'how'; in this case, how to structure the procurement of military manpower. After four weeks I felt I reasonably understood Selective Service. The dominant fact was the huge pool of eligible men, from which only a few had to be selected. So Selective Service was about how to defer the remainder. Married men and students were exempted. Calls were based on the number of men available after deferment: In theory a local board willing to defer everybody would receive no calls. The draft was in fact a lottery; just rigged. And not the way the media believed. The Army did not want the Category 4s and 5s; poorly-educated or with bad records. It wanted and it took the good solid high-school graduates from small towns in the Middle West. I have always thought it was no accident that the political protest in the '70s against the Viet Nam war came so largely from South Dakota, Minnesota, Wisconsin and Iowa.

My report suggested Henry recommend an honest lottery. I took the draft to Bill Gorham, by then an assistant secretary of Health, Education and Welfare but earlier in the Department of Defense. "Best Congressional statement on the draft I've seen", he said. Unhappily, I failed to help Reuss follow up. But interestingly the draft soon was converted into an honest lottery—before being scrapped in favor of the all-volunteer Army.

My Senate half of the fellowship was in Vice President Humphrey's Capitol Hill office. Humphrey was the administration's liaison to cities. That provided a chance to watch the urban/metropolitan legislation. In 1965-66 the Johnson administration was going for a national urban policy, arguing that nobody was balancing the development of the suburbs and the re-development of the inner core, and that this omission was a national problem.

Bill Brussat in the Budget Bureau took me to the Press Club for Robert Weaver's appearance after becoming the first Secretary of Housing and Urban Development. The card on which I'd written my question was the last one read. "Sometimes I hear you say 'city' and you clearly mean the central city; like, New York City. Sometimes you seem to be referring to the urban region." Weaver scratched his head and said: "I guess we are kind of confused about that".

The administration built its bill around the COG idea—regional planning by local elected officials. The strategy was to require each metropolitan area to have a body composed of sitting officials of local jurisdictions, charged to develop a regional plan. All requests for federal aid would be reviewed by this body to ensure the projects were consistent with the regional plan. From this process, we were assured, orderly metropolitan development would proceed.

I kept in touch with the Citizens League work back home; met with Minnesotans when they came to Washington; talked a lot with the ACIR. We were all convinced the COG idea was a wrong 'how'; that it could never resolve controversy where real interests conflicted. *An 'elected' official is one elected to the seat in which s/he is voting.*

I had passed on this conclusion to Minneapolis' congressman, Don Fraser, and when the Model Cities and Metropolitan Development bill came to the House floor he got the requirement for a council of governments amended to say, "except as otherwise provided by state law". That was to prove critical to Minnesota's metropolitan strategy.

"Except as otherwise provided by state law"

I could have stayed on with Reuss, but I wanted to go back to the Star and Tribune, with the metropolitan questions coming up for action.

Minnesota's decision on a regional redesign

The question in late 1966 was how to get the metropolitan policy right in Minnesota.

On our way home from Washington I had gone out in Midge's parents' back yard in Muncie and typed out a memo proposing a Special Council on Areawide Needs (SCAN). It laid out a plan for regional operating organizations coordinated by an elected metro council. Once home I showed it to Verne. "So comprehensive, and looks so far ahead", he said. The League was just then starting a committee to look at metropolitan issues and he felt, I'm sure, that circulation was premature.

In September we went to Ten Mile with a friend, Lu McCarty. Bob Renner, Walker's state representative, and his wife came out for dinner. Bob and I fired up the grill outside while the others talked. I went through the idea for a regional council. "Those of us outside the Twin Cities area will have to do it", Bob said. "You people in the metro area can never agree." This proved prophetic. In the end legislators from 'greater Minnesota' did understand that maintaining the economic, political and social health of the state's major metropolitan region was a priority state interest.

I wrote a second series for the editorial page. A coalition was forming: the League of Metropolitan Municipalities, the Minneapolis Chamber of Commerce, the Upper Midwest Council, the Metropolitan Planning Commission, the League of Women Voters. A conference at the College of St. Thomas showed a consensus on key elements for a regional entity.

Mayors were critically important; especially and encouragingly, the suburban. The city manager in Bloomington, Ray Olsen, was outstanding but what happened would not have succeeded had the suburbs been represented entirely by the professional managers. It was critical to have the mayors, who did not have their professional careers and incomes at stake. This taught a lesson that was to come back later with the debates about restructuring education. School districts have no elected leadership comparable to the mayor in municipal government.

As the Citizens League committee began work in late fall a major issue appeared quickly: whether a metropolitan council should be, as came to be said, an 'operating' body or a 'coordinating' body. In the final report the 'operating' concept prevailed.

During the '67 legislative session the Star and Tribune followed the metro issues closely, urging the Legislature to act. Two metropolitan legislators, Harmon Ogdahl and Bill Frenzel, had a bill for an elected council. Through the session Verne hosted discussions Sunday nights in his basement, at which Ogdahl and Frenzel, key League actives and, importantly, (in a demonstration of consensus politics) Martin Sabo from the DFL reviewed developments and talked about strategies. I sat in, as did Pete Vanderpoel who was getting onto page one of the Pioneer Press stories about what legislators were saying and thinking that day; almost inconceivable today.

At a key House hearing the leadership of the Upper Midwest Council—the CEO of Dayton-Hudson, the president of the First National Bank of Saint Paul and the CEO of Northern States Power Company— came and stayed; simply watched and listened. That quiet signal of support from the business community caused Senator Rosenmeier to respond in days with a bill for a council—with members serving at-large and appointed by the governor. The appearance of that second bill was decisive, turning the question from 'whether' to 'which', meaning something would pass.

Arguments continued about the form the new regional arrangement would take. A suburban representative, Salisbury Adams, thought the regional programs would be adequately handled by independent special districts. Our editorials partly agreed; said the need was not to abolish their existence—only their independence. They should be under a council—as on any major project there is an architect and a general contractor to coordinate the sub-contractors that do the work.

At the Capitol one afternoon I was urging on Adams the need for a politically representative and responsible council to develop a regional consensus that would permit the Legislature to act. In walked his officemate and colleague, Al France from Duluth. I took a chance; asked Al: "Why hasn't the Legislature been able to act on these regional problems all these years?" Immediately he said: "Because you people here can't agree". I turned to Adams: "So give us a council that can get you an agreement."

The session came down to its final days with the two bills deadlocked. Verne and I went out for coffee after session with Renner, chairing the House Committee on Civil Administration. "Pass both bills", Bob said. He did generate such a version. But in the end Frenzel worked the final compromise: a bill calling for a council only, with members appointed by the governor but from equal-population districts (Senate districts combined by twos). The 'operating' issues were left for the 1969 session, with the new council charged first to come in with a solution for a sewerage system. Governor LeVander signed the bill, after motions on the floor to make the council elective failed narrowly. The Star's editorial was headed: "Two Cheers".

The legislation was, as usual, about the halfway mark. The next question was the appointments. LeVander's executive secretary, Dave Durenberger, hinted the chair would be well qualified, having served on both the airports commission and on Metropolitan Planning Commission. That sounded great: It had to be Clayton LeFevere. But LeFevere said, "It's not me". Who, then?

A search of the records showed one other person having held both seats; a person never known as a supporter of the regional idea. Verne's response was for the League to issue a statement simply listing criteria for a council chairman. These of course called for a demonstrated record of support for the metropolitan idea. LeVander then appointed Jim Hetland, long a metro supporter (and past Citizens League president). At the council's first meeting, on the question of its office location, Jim—a Minneapolis resident—broke the tie in favor of Saint Paul. Bob Jorvig, by then Minneapolis city coordinator and probably the area's leading urban professional, was hired to be executive director. The Metropolitan Council was in business.

Going to the Citizens League

That summer, 1967, Verne went to General Mills to head its corporate planning. The League sent Len Ramberg to recruit me to be his successor.

Initially I declined. My work at the newspaper was going well. I was beginning to get into national issues. Bob Smith had me attending meetings of the Editorial Writers Association; getting me beyond urban problems. I was included in the 'civic dining room' lunches occasionally when candidates and visiting dignitaries came to talk with the executives and editors. Senator Eugene McCarthy came; seemed bored by questions about policy; at the end turned to the publisher and said, "John, you don't get things done for Minnesota by changing your representation in Washington every two years." Hubert Humphrey had come earlier, shortly after returning from Europe. He was bubbling over with the concept he'd picked up from those building the new European institutions, about "the necessary in-competence of the politician". All the experts knew it couldn't be done. It was done . . . by politicians who, not being 'competent' in these matters, didn't know it couldn't be done.

In the Spring of 1964 I'd been sent on a swing through the South ahead of the Freedom Summer. I found the Taconic Foundation everywhere. In Jackson, Mississippi Carl Black took me to a motel one evening where people from the National Council of Churches were negotiating— with Senator Stennis' son—the terms on which the young people would be received.

But my interest in urban policy was continuing. And just then Star and Tribune management decided to split the editorial page staff; half to work for each paper. I thought this was not positive. So I told Bob Smith I was leaving, and said yes to Len—who had meantime raised the offer to $19,000.

The job at the League was to stay involved as the Legislature set up the operating side of the metropolitan structure. And to implement the plan Verne had developed to turn the League into a fully metropolitan organization.

This means it is time to talk about the League, which by that time had become quite a remarkable organization.

CHAPTER 6:

The Citizens League

The process this organization developed for thinking about problems—for analyzing the 'why' and recommending the 'how', for proposing effective and realistic solutions—was important to the Twin Cities area and to the state in the years after about 1957. It was able to ask the questions it's not popular to ask, to re-set the issues in controversy and to build support for ideas initially not thought 'realistic'. It was made possible by the contribution of citizen volunteers and by sustaining financing from business firms acting in their civic capacity.

Dan Elazar, a political scientist, a native of Minneapolis, had identified Minnesota as having "a culture of the commonwealth"; which meant all of us together—at that time mostly Yankees and Scandinavians, sharing largely the same values—building a community. In the 1930s, though, that culture deteriorated. There was an overspill of racketeering from Chicago. Teamsters and businessmen from the Citizens Alliance battled in the market during the truck strikes. In 1936 Fortune illustrated its article about the decline of 'the Northwest' with gloomy ink drawings.

A revival began in 1938 with Harold Stassen becoming governor at 31. During the 1940s small 'good government' groups began meeting in Minneapolis. In 1943 the Jaycees led the effort for the Metropolitan Airports Commission. Younger business people and lawyers were coming up. Humphrey ran for mayor; unsuccessfully in '43, successfully in '45. With strong business support the police department was cleaned up, and a start made on clearing Minneapolis' reputation for anti-Semitism.

The failure of the effort in 1948 had not diminished the interest in charter reform. In 1951 Les Park and others decided that Minneapolis needed a permanent civic organization. They looked at the model in Cleveland and elsewhere; in 1952 created a Citizens League (an unfortunate name, given labor's recollection of the Citizens Alliance). It hired Ray Black as executive director. An effort to rate and endorse candidates was quickly dropped. The League set up the usual standing committees; sent staff with yellow pencils to track the city budget. Issued reports; made recommendations. The first was for a sprinkler system in Minneapolis General Hospital. Gradually its skills improved. In 1957 the League was effective with the proposal for the Legislature to authorize a park system for Hennepin County.

Verne Johnson

In 1958 Ray left; Verne Johnson came in and created the process responsible for the organization's later success. He had been briefly a lawyer; had served a term in the House; had worked in Young Republican politics, playing a lead role in organizing the write-in for Eisenhower in 1952. In 1958 he was in Washington, an assistant to Minneapolis Congressman Walter Judd.

Verne changed the process; dropping the standing committees in favor of study committees recruited for particular assignments. From the lawyers the League took the format for its reports. Findings; important, but not enough. Conclusions; the 'should', also important but also not enough. There must be an 'order for judgment', a recommendation that contains a 'how' that answers the question legislators ask: "What is it you want me to do?".

Verne had strong ties with younger people from his political world; worked closely with the new legislators then getting elected in Hennepin County. His political sense told him to think in terms of what legislators would find in their interest. He did not, like most reformers, talk to elected officials about the need to do good. He showed them how doing good could work to their political benefit. Had he been involved in the discussion about education policy in the '80s, for example, he would probably have been less inclined to lecture them about family choice than to show legislators how their own goals were frustrated by the public-utility arrangement that made the district system unresponsive to the state's felt need for change.

Verne had outstanding skills. He had a sense that successful organizations have a clear central mission; that they rise or decline, never stay the same. And that success with proposals requires having "a simple central message". He was frustrated by those who could not see the essentials: "Some things are *too* obvious", he would say. He knew the importance of 'thought leaders' and knew who they were. He was firm in his conviction that "more change comes through challenge than through consensus". If he saw a committee becoming too challenging, however, he would counsel realism. If he saw one thinking too politically, he would push it to be more 'imaginative'. "Orchestrating off imbalances", was his term for this. He was careful, as he would say in private, to "lead without seeming to lead". (No Citizens League executive director said "My board".) He would give a group not two but three alternatives; positioning the one he wanted in the middle, knowing that most groups will settle on the center. He had a strong sense for the way 'most people' think. Rather than disagree directly with a statement he thought wrong, he would restate the other person's assertion in such a way as to cause that person to disagree with himself. At the 7:30 Tuesday breakfasts, which became the best issue discussions in town, Verne usually asked the last and best question.

"Some things are too obvious"

The League's work was not solicited by the entity under study and sometimes not welcomed. Committees asked questions; got answers.

Gradually the level of knowledge and sophistication in the active membership rose. Increasingly the committees asked what was *causing* problems; came to understand how structure caused systems to work as they did; came to see policy action as getting the system incentives right. At times the League came in at the end of the game to 'kick the winning field goal' with a politically skillful and broadly acceptable compromise. But increasingly it was opening new areas; clarifying the problems.

It was important to be a group advocating a civic rather than a private agenda. The League's influence came from having members who were both knowledgeable and dis-interested. This was unusual: Everywhere there are people who know what is going on but whose roles and positions constrain their candor; everywhere there are people eager to offer their opinions who do not know or entirely understand what is really going on. Out of the League process came citizens with a good combination of both.

I came to believe this work of citizens, amateurs, was better and more effective than that of professional consultants. The paid consultant is unlikely to tell the client what the client does not want to hear or is not inclined to do. With no client relationship, with financing from others, the League was in a position to say what needed to be said; to sharpen on the problems and their causes.

Those in the public sector working for change came to appreciate this. "I work with the League", said Bill Frenzel, later congressman, "because they give me better information than I can get anywhere else." At a critical point in the debate about the hospital system a leading administrator said: "These issues had been festering inside our closed community of professionals. You guys open the window, let the fresh air in". Others talked about the reports 'throwing light' on a problem. "We had people who *knew* the school-finance problem," one of Wendell Anderson's advisers was to say to me in 1971 (see Chapter 10). "We just didn't *see* it."

The League begins to make things happen

The creation of the Hennepin County Park Reserve District was a major accomplishment in Ray Black's time. The second (after the failure of the 1960 charter campaign) was the referendum in 1962 on the capital-improvement program for Minneapolis schools.

Up to 1957 the district's borrowing for buildings had to run through the City Council. It got approval to build new elementary schools in the corners of the city being developed after 1950. But the coming issue was re-building: The last big capital program had been in the 1920s. Frustrated by Alderman Moulton's restrictive borrowing program, the school board in 1957 persuaded the Legislature to free it from City Council control. But its borrowing still required a vote of the people.

A proposed capital program was to go on the ballot in September '62. The League took it under study. It found the proposal a *rehabilitation* program: a new wing on every building; something for everybody, a plan designed simply to get votes for the bond issue, dealing with none of the real problems about the size and location of buildings. Minneapolis at that time had five high schools across the city south of downtown: Vocational, West, Central, South and Marshall.

The League proposed a *replacement* program: Close whole schools; sell off the sites; build new schools at new sites. It first tried to persuade the school board to reconsider. The board declined; confident it had support from business and its traditional civic allies. Opposition would be unwelcome. Verne wrote a compelling brief for the case against approval. The League board took a deep breath and, confident in the logic of its case for replacement, decided to take the issue to the people. Vote 'no', it recommended.

On the editorial page we supported the League's reasoning, and in the election the proposal was defeated. Quickly the League suggested the board get a second opinion. A survey team from Michigan State was retained. It agreed with the League's recommendation for a replacement program. The proposal was re-cast and resubmitted. The League urged a 'yes' vote. The bonding program was approved. So in the mid-'60s

Minneapolis was building new schools in its oldest neighborhoods: a new North High, a new South. West, Central and Marshall were soon closed.

The experience taught the League that cities' and school districts' need for voter approval offered opportunities to get changes in the public interest. On several occasions the League said it could support a 'yes' vote if, *prior to the election*, the board would commit to levy only some part of the increase allowed, or to use the revenue in some particular way. The lesson was: Never trade money for promises. Get a commitment, in writing.

Never trade money for promises

After that, and after the 1963 legislative session that began to modernize Hennepin County government, the League moved rapidly into metropolitan affairs. In a series of study committees it looked at particular service fields; developing the case for coordination and overall policy direction incorporated in the legislation in 1967.

Public-finance issues had come along, as well. The *Dulton* case touched off a re-valuation of property taxes. In Minneapolis the League was instrumental in setting criteria that led to Gordon Moe's appointment as city assessor. Its work with the sales tax question, by a committee co-chaired by John Mooty and David Graven, played a major role in Minnesota's decision in 1967 to add a sales tax as the 'third leg' to the revenue system. (See Chapter 8.)

It was at this point that I came to work there.

1967: Picking up the metropolitan issues

The first job was to pick up the metropolitan question; the Legislature having left for later the larger questions about the structure of the regional operating systems. There was now a regional council, but still independent special districts or other arrangements for sewerage, airports, transit, etc. Our question was what to say about this to the 1969 session.

The Metro Council itself went to work on a solution for the sewerage problem. Minneapolis and Saint Paul opposed a metropolitan system; arguing to maintain their joint ownership and the contract arrangement. The Council proposed a regional system it would plan, own and operate. Legislators asked the cities: Did you get a fair hearing? City representatives allowed that they had. That was enough. The Legislature voted for a metropolitan system. It did not, however, accept the Metropolitan Council's proposal that it should itself be the regional organization building and operating the interceptors and treatment plants. It created a separate Metropolitan Waste Control Commission, charged to build and run the system.

Coming into the session the League had re-thought the question of the operating vs. coordinating arrangement, in a committee chaired by Greer Lockhart. The League proposed to extend the system of regional service commissions, separate from but subordinate to the council; their members appointed by and their plans and finances approved by the Council. The 'three golden threads', as Dave Graven put it. The idea was to concentrate the Council's attention on policy-making; on key regional decisions rather than on administrative operations.

The 1969 Legislature gave the council some greater planning authority for the existing regional special districts: the Metropolitan Airports Commission, then considering a second major airport, and the Metropolitan Transit Commission, which had been made statutory.

So by mid-1969 the framework for the metropolitan level was basically set—quite a different answer than in other states to the 'how' of regional arrangements. Not a council of governments. Not direct state operation. Not a growing set of un-coordinated special districts. Not a consolidated regional 'municipality'. The Council not an operating body. It was neither state nor local, said the attorney general's opinion, but an entity lying intermediate between the two and possessing some of the attributes of each. It was a regional council set up on the 'one person/ one vote' principle and with some real opportunity to act as the architect and 'general contractor' on the job of metropolitan development.

But . . . also not elected. Which was to prove a serious matter.

Legislative reorganization and other matters

The League's proposal for legislative reorganization was accepted by the 1969 Legislature; the idea that it meet each year of the biennium but only for 120 days and in the first five months of each year. (See Chapter 11.) It was another of those delightful cases where a League volunteer took charge of a legislative committee discussion; Kristine Johnson tactfully explaining to Senator Gearty the difference between his bill and the bill from Senator McCutcheon. The contrast was striking with other organizations that sent a staff member to read a statement.

On the finance front, Rep. Weaver's bill carrying our proposal for sharing the growth of the commercial-industrial tax base (see Chapter 9) passed the House and was waiting action in the Senate when the session ran out.

That June I went to England for a conference at Ditchley on "Citizen Participation in Urban Planning", an idea for which the chair, Duncan Sandys, was notably restrained in his enthusiasm. On the terrace one afternoon I ran through the 1967-69 Minnesota legislative developments with Bill Slayton, former head of the federal Housing and Home Finance Agency. "I don't believe it", he said.

Several of those at Ditchley were individuals in the group of "metropolitan affairs nonprofit corporations" (MANCs): John Keith from Regional Plan Association of New York, Angelo Siracusa from the Bay Area Council, Bob Pease from the Allegheny Conference in Pittsburgh, Homer Wadsworth from the Kansas City Association of Trusts and Foundations, Kent Mathewson, by this time at the Metropolitan Fund in Detroit, among others. Working with plans, grants or community influence, most were different than the League, a citizen-based group working with ideas.

Tom Anding had graciously turned over to me his place in that network. The once-a-year, informal, slowly-round-the-table discussions—at places like Rolling Rock—gave an inside look at the problems, efforts and developments in each urban region. They were enormously informative, too, about different ways of getting things done.

The League becomes a metropolitan organization

Verne had left a plan for the League to broaden into a fully metro-politan organization. Recognizing the support in Saint Paul for a zoo, different and better than its municipal Como Zoo, he pushed to program a study for a new state zoo, with the thought it might locate in the East Metro. He recruited Saint Paul people for this and other study committees.

Saint Paul was a challenge. Strong local institutions still wanted to keep separate from Minneapolis: the Chamber of Commerce; the Saturday brunch at the Minnesota Club where business executives talked over what Saint Paul should do on civic affairs. Gradually, it came along. Phil Nason helped, at the First National Bank; Waverly Smith at the St. Paul Companies. Our breakfasts in downtown Saint Paul began to draw.

We had also to continue the work on the metropolitan agenda, where a new challenge was emerging. Absorbed with its new respon-sibilities, the Metropolitan Council had not noticed the MTC racing ahead with its plans for a rail transit system. This was to present the next big question about the 'how' of a major system in the region. It was one of several system issues that would also occupy the Citizens League in the decade ahead.

CHAPTER 7:

Rethinking Urban Transportation

The 1970s saw the region in a long and intense debate, trying to think out a sensible transportation policy; especially, the role of public vehicles in a transportation system now consisting largely of private vehicles. At the League we were quickly drawn in.

Roads and freeways

Though Minneapolis and Saint Paul were built in the streetcar era, most of the Twin Cities region as it existed in 1970 was built in the auto era. Lower-density development, plus the zoning that separated residential areas from commercial areas, created a huge demand for travel and so for an expanded system of roads.

The Interstate Highway program in 1956 was sold as a national system connecting major urban regions. But it was intended also to relieve congestion within the urban regions, improving access to their central areas.

Trouble appeared in key cities as the discussions about route location and design began. Engineers whose career had been building rural roads were unprepared for the issues they met in the cities. Quickly controversies flared: from San Francisco to Boston. Serious resistance in the media and among city planners came to focus at the anti-freeway Hartford Conference as early as 1956. In the 1960s the executive director of AASHO, the American Association of State Highway Officials, Alf Johnson, was in state after state telling engineers that if they did not adapt, the planning of urban roads would be taken away from them.

During the strike in 1962 the Guild, the reporters, went out in support of the Teamsters. It was not good to be out of work for five months, especially with son Alan about to arrive. Sam Romer, I think, found us temporary jobs in state government. I worked in the planning section of the Highway Department; got to know Deane Wenger and Don Carroll, in charge of the studies underlying the freeway system planning.

The early Highway Department plan for the Interstate system in our region was pretty crude: The document simply squared off the outer circumferential on the west to fit the map onto the page. The actual system planning that led to route locations and interchange designs was based on origin/destination studies, adapting the earlier Chicago Area Transportation Study (CATS) to our region as TCATS. Find what land uses would be located where, ask people where they wanted to go from where they lived, and the computer would calculate 'desire lines' of travel over which freeways would be located (much as colleges in the East paved sidewalks over the paths students actually walked).

The System 5 computer run was showing a need for seven freeways into downtown Minneapolis. That was bound to be a hard sell.

Significant controversies arose where the neighbors were influential: in Southeast Minneapolis, for example. The proposal was for I-94 to cross the river near the University of Minnesota campus—which meant it would run through a neighborhood where many vocal University of Minnesota people lived. They wanted a crossing farther south, at 26th Street. Governor Orville Freeman ended the debate by ordering the piers sunk in the river at Dartmouth Avenue—near the campus.

The Department did not get much help. For a time the Tribune's Civic Progress column explained the designs and the controversies, but these ended when Dan Upham retired. From that point on the Highway Department was on its own, hurt by its inability to spend road-user money for public information. In the hearings about projects the engineers were overmatched: Officials in even the smallest municipality felt themselves superior simply because they were elected.

In the end the Twin Cities area got a good system: a fairly large network of fairly small freeways with parallel arterials to take the overflow. By the early 1970s the decisions were pretty well made.

The need remained, nationally, for better decision-making arrangements. Kurt Bauer in Milwaukee invited me to several of the meetings at which 'the highway lobby' struggled with the problem of how to get approvals at both the system and project levels; memorably, four days at the Mount Pocono conference. Auto manufacturers were not terribly concerned: Though initially troubled by the opposition at the Hartford Conference, they soon realized that so long as suburbs continued to develop in the pattern of single-family homes the demand for cars and roads was assured. Officials who actually had to site the roads were more active in the search for more effective decision-making arrangements.

At bottom—as Anthony Downs explained most clearly—traffic congestion is an inescapable feature of modern urban life, so long as people can choose where to live, work and shop, prefer large-lot subdivisions and enjoy the privacy of traveling alone. Because widening the freeways improves travel times, improvements there attract more cars: At rush hour the freeways will always be full. The net effect of increasing freeway capacity is to reduce traffic on the parallel arterial streets.

Perhaps the transportation system most used by the people of a region always becomes a target for criticism. I remember how in Omaha we disliked the streetcars. Today, when almost everyone drives, it is popular to regard the automobile as an evil. Normally—at a restaurant, in a church on Sunday, in a political meeting or at a concert—'full' is a sign of success. Not so, for roads. I stood one afternoon with a small group high up in Galtier Towers in downtown Saint Paul, looking at the river of red tail-lights flowing north on I-35E in the afternoon rush-hour.

"Isn't that awful!" was the general reaction; as if being filled with moving vehicles the freeway was not a success. Perhaps this is the influence of the television ads, always showing you in your car alone on the road, cruising home along the leafy suburban street or speeding along the cliff above the ocean.

The anti-auto ethic soon combined with the talk about 'congestion' to revive discussion about transit. It was to generate a controversy that ran for years, raising in the most difficult way the questions about the 'why' and 'how' of ways for people to get around. But that debate produced some important insights as we thought about what 'transit' is and how to introduce a new concept of it.

Beyond streetcars and buses

I came to Minneapolis just at the end of the streetcar era. It was a system focused on the two downtowns; lines every six blocks so workers and shoppers needed to walk at most three. In the '50s the streetcars were sold to Mexico City, replaced by buses. Even with the bus, the public-vehicle business—scheduled service on fixed routes—was a bad business. All over America bus systems were collapsing.

About 1960 a group of Minneapolis businessmen bought Twin City Lines. The night the story broke, Dave Lee, writing it for the business page, sat back to back with me in the newsroom. The managing editor was looking over Dave's shoulder, the executive editor was looking over the managing editor's shoulder and the publisher was looking over the executive editor's shoulder as Dave typed. It got crowded.

A few years later the new owners were asking the public to buy them out. The idea was not to turn this losing business into a good business. The idea was to move it from private to public ownership, using the Metropolitan Transit Commission (MTC) created in 1966. Jack Doolittle was soon brought in from Boston to be its head, replacing a director embarrassed by photos of his three-car garage. The MTC did buy the bus system. Some wondered quietly why the public should pay anything for an organization with pension liabilities exceeding the value of its assets. But the condemnation went through. The public was in the transit business.

After that the question became: "What's transit?" Initially it was better bus service: "We're getting there!" the MTC ads jingled. But the MTC had bigger ideas.

The Metropolitan Council, busy setting up the sewerage system and wrestling with the question of a second airport, in 1972 suddenly realized the MTC was seriously going to propose a rail system in the coming legislative session. My God, the Council realized: The system plan is our job. And we have no plan!

Immediately the Council set out to get itself a transit plan. Out of a meeting at the Sheraton Ritz hotel came a contract to Dick Braun, then at Barton-Aschman, beginning a process that recommended a program of bus on freeway.

The MTC declined to be guided by the Council's plan. So the issue was joined in the '73 legislative session. Into the discussion came other ideas, however; as, 'personalized rapid transit' (PRT) and a fundamentally different definition of 'transit'.

The puzzle: What's 'transit'?

The next three years saw an intensive debate—a contentious but quite sophisticated policy discussion—intensified by the arrival in 1973 of the shortage of, and the rise in price of, petroleum. Several ideas came into play.

Busway—This was the Metro Council preference: separate rights-of-way for buses and other multi-passenger vehicles that could also move onto surface streets. In 1975 a specific proposal came from the task force Mayor Hofstede had asked to develop transit on Hiawatha Avenue in Minneapolis. That proposal for a reserved right-of-way would have gotten multi-passenger vehicles out of the auto stream. Hiawatha was not a corridor of interest to the MTC, but the light-rail advocates killed the proposal, anyway: Their strategy has always been to remove all competing proposals, leaving the transit question one of 'yes' or 'no' on LRT.

Rail—In the '70s 'rail' meant something like the Bay Area Rapid Transit (BART) or the commuter systems in big eastern cities. Wayne Thompson, who had come from Oakland, California to head public affairs for Dayton-Hudson Corporation, was pushing this approach. (Wayne shuddered at the idea of 'light' rail.) So the MTC kept plugging 'fixed-guideway'—meaning vehicles fixed *to* the guideway—in corridors connecting the downtowns with suburban commercial centers. Advocates took public officials on trips to see such 'real' transit. Jon Schroeder, on the Citizens League staff, went on one of these trips; on return wrote a candid account of this high-level lobbying. Too candid. I suppressed it.

Personal Rapid Transit—Lloyd Berggren and Ed Anderson, inventors, pitched the idea of taking the 'mass' out of transit; proposed PRT, an automated system with the characteristics of the auto; a private ride, origin to destination. The Senate committee was interested, but the technology was obviously not in being and the idea did not sell.

The 'internal circulator'—Dick Wolsfeld, a key consultant, suggested deploying fixed-guideway as an 'internal circulator' *within* the two 'metro centers'; in Minneapolis, for example, connecting the business district with the arts-and-cultural area to the southwest, with the University to the east and with other adjacent high-activity centers. It would have had a subway under Sixth Street. People would come to the metro center by bus or car, transfer or park, and then distribute around the central area on the circulator. In George Latimer's time as mayor of Saint Paul the internal circulator got seriously considered there. But the light-rail people killed that too.

Light Rail—As the other options were set aside the rail fans, streetcar buffs and county officials began to push light rail. They had bided their time, knowing they would get little hearing while commuter and BART-type rail were alive. Once these came off the agenda light rail would be the only rail; would be the only 'real transit'. Only the busway and ride-sharing ideas stood in their way.

By 1976, frustrated and exhausted, the Legislature and Metro Council dismissed both BART and PRT; settled on bus-on-freeway. The light-rail people were quiet. For a time.

The Citizens League's answer: Transit is riding

Clearly the subject cried out for good thinking; for a reappraisal of the simplistic notion that transit is defined in vehicle terms and that 'real transit' is vehicles with steel wheels fixed to rails laid out in corridors.

As committees of the League began to dig into the question some of the realities began to appear. Investment strategies and pricing questions mattered. Our committee had a wonderful meeting one night with the MTC and engineers from the power company and the telephone company about how to provide service for the 'peak hour' problem; how these other utilities priced service on- and off-peak. It was always useful to look across system boundaries.

Paul Gilje did a wonderful job generating the essential numbers. These were important.

Ours is a low-density region with two major centers about eight miles apart; so is a 12-corridor region. (Chicago by contrast, on the Lake Michigan shore, is a three-corridor city; Honolulu a one-corridor city.)

The 'modal split' was dramatic. Here all forms of conventional transit combined carried roughly three per cent of the region's daily trips. The area could double or triple that and not make a significant dent on petroleum usage, air pollution or traffic congestion. Both our problems and the solutions to them lay in the way we used the automobile.

Conventional thinking looked to build transit by increasing density. It forgot about propinquity. Density means little if the people living in the apartments and condos all want to go different places. And people do not necessarily work where they live. Persuading people not to drive would require nonstop service to and from home.

In a low-density region rail could not do that. (One consultant, from Philadelphia, said he lived on a quarter-acre lot within a 15-minute walk of the train. No doubt he did. But simple arithmetic showed that not very many people can live on quarter-acre lots a 15-minute walk from the station.) Nor could the bus, legally or practically: residential streets cannot handle its weight. Only a vehicle like the car can get people to and from home.

The League proposal for transit facilities was, as a result, one for reserved right-of-way open to multi-passenger vehicles *not* fixed to the guideway. Roads, bridges, parking facilities should be adapted, we said, to give preference to multi-passenger vehicles. We liked Dick Wolsfeld's proposal to use fixed-guideway in/around the metro centers, putting it where the auto truly could not compete, using it to build the urban core.

On the service side, our proposal was that public policy treat all vehicles as transit vehicles; define a 'transit development program' as essentially "Building Incentives for Drivers to Ride"— the title of one report. In the context of the oil crisis during the '70s this made basic sense. Were the petroleum flow to be turned off, the region would surely rearrange the private vehicle fleet to carry passengers.

A new form of ridesharing appeared about 1973; developed by Bob Owens. He had left the Highway Department to be transportation director at 3M Company. Bob crossed a bus with a carpool, producing a hybrid called the 'commuter van'. An employee got a 12-passenger van to drive others to work; could keep the fares from the last three passengers and had the vehicle for personal use evenings and weekends. Chrysler picked up the program for multi-employer centers.

A 'transit development program' as essentially "Building Incentives for Drivers to Ride"

The new concepts stirred the MTC to some demonstrations. It tried small-vehicle and dial-a-ride services. All failed; perhaps were designed to fail. Then Carolyn Rodriguez, a freshman state representative, got through 'opt-out' legislation that let 'someone else' try. Suburbs at the end of the bus line could withdraw, keep 90 per cent of the tax levy they had been sending to the MTC and use those dollars to finance a program designed for their own residents' needs. That worked; still operates.

Busways did not develop during this period. The federal-aid program did not then finance reserved right-of-way for multi-passenger vehicles.

Later, when commissioner of transportation, Dick Braun got a high-occupancy-vehicle lane into I-394 and worked an arrangement with Mike Christenson, when Mike was head of the MTC, to use the outside 'reaction lane' in the freeways as a sort-of exclusive lane for buses.

Beyond claiming that conventional transit would reduce congestion, advocates said fixed-guideway transit would 'shape development'. I remember at a conference one consultant comparing the effect of a rail line to the effect of a bar magnet set on a table covered with iron filings. That was extreme, but as time went on it was clear that a major objective was to use transit to change land-uses along the line.

In 1979, on becoming chair of the MTC, John Yngve found a bus system seriously neglected and an agency distracted by the endless warfare over some not-bus system. He and Lou Olsen, the general manager, got serious about the cost problems—including the rule that no one could become a bus driver without working first as a bus washer.

In some ways the critical thing missing was an institution that could think across the modes; could integrate facilities (roads and vehicles) with non-capital strategies. A Regional Transportation Board was set up in the 1980s to do essentially that, but it was captured by the light-rail interests. In time the counties emerged to claim the lead role and transit became again a purely 'facilities' question.

Also, after 1980, concerns about the price and availability of petroleum receded. The economy was in recession. And a Republican governor, Al Quie, was in office. So the 'transit' issue was set aside.

Looking back now, from 2021, it seems increasingly clear that the Citizens League work on transit saw fundamentals correctly.

The automobile fleet was then and still is the largest carrier of riders; far larger than the transit system. The roads were congested with cars themselves basically empty; the five-passenger vehicle usually carrying a driver only. So the automobile fleet had the capacity to be an even larger transit system; 'transit' defined as *riding*.

A transit development program, then, would be a utilization strategy; an effort to push up the proportion of riders relative to drivers. Including the automobile as a transit vehicle made sense also because such a high proportion of trips begin or end at home, and because our area 'home' so largely means single-family houses. *The best transit system therefore is the one best able to get people nonstop to and from home.*

Ridesharing included the taxi business. Traditionally selling an exclusive ride, taxis clearly could offer a 'group ride' (all passengers to one destination) or, as in Washington DC, a 'shared ride' (different passengers to different destinations). We saw the limousine business, the charter bus business, the rental-car business, all as part of the transit system; all selling rides. We also noted the appearance, in Pittsburgh, of the 'occasional taxi'—an arrangement that allowed owners of a private car to check in, at a time of high demand, to accept riders. Recently of course this idea has reappeared in a far more significant way as Uber and Lyft.

In the 1980s political people took the transit discussion away from planners; the counties went into LRT development. In the mid-'90s the Metropolitan Council accepted the idea of rail lines in return for the counties agreeing to busways.

As of 2021 the picture remains mixed. Central city councils promote biking and higher-density development. Light rail lines continue to develop, while concern rises about its on-board safety and about the billions a line now costs. Manufacturers are going electric rapidly. The self-driving car seems a ways away, but quite possibly fewer people will be owning cars; more will be buying rides. In an urban region where the homes and other destinations are widely dispersed, and continually changing, the successful 'transit system' still seems likely to be the one able to deliver a non-stop ride.

Meantime . . .

In recounting these debates about metropolitan affairs I have skipped past the League's work on another big system: public finance. It is time now to go back and pick up this question, which had started to become a high-visibility issue in the late '60s.

SECTION THREE:

FINDING THE 'HOW' IN FINANCE

In the 1960s several developments were building pressure for a substantial redesign of Minnesota's system of public finance. The *Dulton* case forced assessors first to value all classes of property at market, then apply Minnesota's statutory classification. And business personal property was taken off the rolls. On the editorial page we tried to explain especially the new approach to valuation.

By the mid-'60s the state was increasingly challenged to finance its growing responsibilities. In the 1930s when many states went to a sales tax Minnesota had gone to the income tax—as Governor Olson won his battle with Senator Rockne. So in the '60s the question was whether to add the tax on sales as the 'the third leg' of the state tax system. The design ques-

77

tions were minor. The big question was how politically to get this done, given the historic objection to the sales tax on equity grounds. The story of that 'how' appears in Chapter 8.

The public-finance system also needed to be adapted to the realities of the new regional definition of the city. A key question was how to make the local property tax compatible with the goals of metropolitan planning. Chapter 9 tells the story of the Citizens League's proposal for sharing the growth of the commercial-industrial base. Adopted in 1971, this attracted national attention; might in some ways be the most remarkable 'how' in this book.

Another major public finance reform came in K-12 education; equalizing and partly relieving the burden of the property tax for schools. In the late '60s serious inequities were causing more and more bond issues and millage increases to fail. A League proposal became the central issue of the gubernatorial campaign in 1970 and the legislative session of 1971, in ways Chapter 10 describes.

In public finance, especially, Minnesota found it possible to introduce innovative—yet implementable—solutions in a field long dominated by the interests of taxpayer groups and of the spending jurisdictions.

CHAPTER 8:

The Sales Tax

Opposition to a tax on sales was rooted in the conviction that it fell most heavily on the necessities of life, so was inherently inequitable and unfair to working people. This had driven Minnesota's decision in the 1930s and was still a central tenet of labor and of the Democratic-Farmer-Labor (DFL) party into the 1960s.

While governor, Orville Freeman had started some reappraisal; had appointed a study commission chaired by Cameron Thomson, CEO of Northwest Bancorporation, with a staff headed by Harvey Brazer of the University of Michigan. Its report in 1956 introduced the idea of a credit to offset the regressivity. Nothing followed, however. The sales tax remained blocked by the old rhetoric in the DFL: Income tax good; sales tax bad.

Pressures intensified into the 1960s. By the middle of the decade the rate of approval for school district bond issues and levies was falling precipitously; the state was being pressed to raise aids for education. Local property taxes were rising toward two percent of market value. Minneapolis' city assessor told me the removal of business inventories and equipment from the tax base took off the rolls the city's largest taxpayer: the mainframe computers of IBM. Pressed by the *Dulton* decision, assessors were having to reduce some commercial valuations.

All this forced local councils to reappraise local budgets. It hit hard on the Iron Range, which had long tapped the valuation of the mining companies, now in decline. An article in the Gilbert Herald described the effect there: The city would no longer mow homeowners' boulevard lawns, could no longer provide maintenance men for city churches; would no longer provide part-time employment for high-school seniors and widows, or plow gardens at city expense.

Into 1965 the DFL opposition to a tax on sales remained intense. After conferring with Governor Rolvaag the party chair, George Farr, wrote that "the sales tax is just as inequitable and unacceptable as it has ever been".

The Star and Tribune editorial page supported broadening the tax base. The idea of a credit remained attractive. An editorial in July '65 picked up on a suggestion by Arthur Naftalin, the DFL mayor of Minneapolis, that the discussion could and should be shifted from the question of source to the question of benefits and burdens.

I had come across a table showing how credits of different sizes would shift the incidence of the tax; showed in an article on the Star opinion page how a credit on 'the necessities of life' could take the regressivity out of a general sales tax. "What this means is that the discussion about a sales tax should, and can, be shifted off the pros and cons of a sales tax in principle, onto a practical basis where agreement can be reached."

Harold LeVander was elected governor in 1966. A Republican, his election might have been expected to improve the prospects for a sales tax. But during the campaign LeVander had committed to oppose the sales tax. So the initiative would have to come from some other direction. And the legislation would have to be passed over his veto. Which of course made it even more important to find the 'how' that would work politically.

Late in 1966 the Citizens League took the question under study. Verne had the committee co-chaired by John Mooty, his longtime friend and a senior Republican active, and Dave Graven, a law professor at the University of Minnesota, a DFLer willing to make 'good government' causes the base for his political ambitions. The report early in 1967 argued the need for the tax, proposed a three per cent rate and advocated the offsetting credit.

Graven made it compelling: No tax *source* is inherently anything: I can construct a regressive income tax on the back of an envelope in two minutes. Everything depends on what's covered, the rates applied and the exemptions or credits provided—and, of course, on the use to which the revenues are put. More politically: Why wouldn't the party most committed to public spending want to see state revenues enlarged when that can be done equitably?

> *No tax* **source** *is inherently anything*

With that understood, the last defense of the DFL old-timers crumbled.

True to his word, LeVander vetoed the bill. The Legislature passed it over his veto. The three-cent tax provided relief for property-tax-payers and some additional revenue for municipalities and for schools. In the end, to keep it simple, legislators used exemptions rather than credits to take out the regressivity: No tax on food and clothing.

The Legislature failed, however, to require that local levies be reduced to reflect the new non-property revenue provided. That let localities and school boards continue their existing levies; the voters not seeing the property-tax relief. Their continuing increases in spending and taxing was to come back four years later in the struggle over education finance.

CHAPTER 9:

Fiscal Disparities and Financing Transit

In 1967 the Twin Cities area had a new regional government. There was a small property levy provided for its own operations. But nothing had been done to redesign the system of local government finance so it would not continue to work at cross purposes with the objective of coherent regional development.

American cities depend heavily on the property tax to finance their services. We hardly notice other nations that do it differently. It was a surprise on the CURA trip to Copenhagen in 1980 to hear its chief planning officer, Kai Lemberg, say: We don't want the corporate office buildings in the city center: They belong in the suburbs. The Netherlands, too, makes little use of the property tax.

We tend not to realize how far the pattern of urban development in our urban regions—the concentration of tall office buildings in our downtowns, for example—is an artifact of our system of local public finance. Here, for local officials, everything depended on getting valuations physically located within their boundaries. To grow its tax base a jurisdiction was inevitably tempted to bend its planning or zoning requirements. Into the 1960s municipalities and school districts in the Twin Cities area were competing for taxable development; running beggar-my-neighbor policies seeking to bring in high-value development and to push onto others the 'unprofitable' development like tract housing.

But even this could not overcome geography and history. Some parts of our region were naturally winners; others not. Those with freeways or near the airport developed a rich tax base so had lower rates and/or better services; others got little tax base so had higher rates and/or poorer services. So the question arose: How to make the local property tax less an impediment to orderly metropolitan growth?

Sharing the commercial/industrial base

By the early 1960s the fiscal implications of metropolitanism were coming up rapidly on the policy agenda. We pointed out that municipal need, and disparity, is an artifact of the governance system. Suppose we converted Minneapolis' 13 wards into 13 municipalities, each required to finance its needs from the property located within its own boundaries. We would be creating new disparities, would we not?

The traditional answers seemed out of reach. One would have been to consolidate; to create larger municipal jurisdictions, broadening the tax base. Or for the state to increase aids to the property-poor municipalities from state revenue sources. Or for state legislation to authorize a regional entity to raise, collect and distribute revenue.

In May 1968 the League put a committee to work thinking about the 'disparity' issues and the perverse incentives the property-tax system created for orderly development. Charles Weaver, a House member from a district in the north suburban (the low value) part of the region, was interested. Curious, I drove to Anoka early in November for lunch with him.

A few days later Weaver wrote the League an important letter. The new Metropolitan Council, he noted, would be making decisions about the location of freeways, transit lines, regional parks and perhaps major commercial centers. In shaping the region it would inescapably be shaping the tax base of the region. These decisions would be easier, better, fairer, he thought, if there were some way to capture and redistribute the revenues from the values created by metropolitan decisions. He suggested a revenue-sharing program, using the taxes (over a certain threshold) from commercial-industrial property to help finance the schools.

In the study committee, however, a private fiscal consultant, Warren Preeshl, suggested sharing not revenue but the tax base itself. No one, anywhere, had seen this possibility. Everyone thought of 'the tax base' as the buildings; immovable. Preeshl saw the tax base as numbers. Numbers can be moved. He and Paul Gilje, on the League staff, worked it out. The committee proposed it; the board adopted it. The idea went out for discussion: "Breaking the Tyranny of the Local Property Tax".

> *Preeshl saw the tax base as numbers. Numbers can be moved*

We had intense discussions with Art Whitney, the influential head of the governments department at the Dorsey office. Art preferred a region-wide levy on commercial-industrial property. Paul and I had a hard time believing the business community would want a direct levy on commercial property. Finally, at a breakfast in the Rand Tower basement, Art said: "If you want to do it (base-sharing), it will work." That was enough.

Weaver picked up the plan; put it into 1969 session. Jack Windhorst, at Dorsey, drafted a skillful (though impenetrable) bill. At the hearing I found myself saying to legislators: Don't try to read the language. We used graphics to explain its process.

Weaver got it through the House. In the Senate, coming down to the final day, with his tax committee scheduled for one last meeting, Senator Donald Wright called around the business community looking for someone to testify in opposition. Fred Cady from Honeywell declined. John Barker from General Mills declined. Wright canceled the meeting, and the session ran out.

So the idea lay over until 1971, when it came up alongside the school finance issue. Nothing happened in the regular session. When the bill came up in the first special session Weaver got it through. It was a fascinating vote; quite rational. Not at all on party lines. Rep. Lon Heinitz, from a well-propertied suburb, told Weaver he planned to vote 'no', but "If you need my vote you'll have it". Conservatives like Salisbury Adams saw equalization diminishing the pressure for spending: Because rich school districts spent more, poor districts were always pressing the Legislature to be equalizing school aids upward.

The new base-sharing program worked entirely with the *growth* of the commercial-industrial base. From and after 1971, 40 per cent of the net increase in non-residential valuations was excluded from entering directly into the tax base of the jurisdiction in which the property was located; was pooled at the seven-county level and redistributed by population, weighted slightly by whether a jurisdiction's residential valuation per capita was above or below the metropolitan average. An area-wide rate was derived; then applied to the area-wide base, which formed some part of the valuation of each commercial/industrial parcel. A key was that in deciding what to levy and spend no taxing jurisdiction could do to its non-voting commercial owners anything it was not willing to do to its voting residential owners.

It was a struggle to get the county auditors to cooperate in the administration. And twice in succeeding years high-value suburbs brought legal challenges. Both times the state Supreme Court upheld the law. Base-sharing has been in effect since, not changed fundamentally despite repeated efforts to subject it to annual legislative gaming. In 2015 Bloomington did win permission to exempt, for a time, a part of the growth in valuation created by the expansion of its huge Mall of America.

In 2017 about one-third of the commercial-industrial taxable value was being shared. The program has narrowed significantly the disparity in commercial-industrial valuations per capita. In 2021 Paul Gilje wrote the full history of this remarkable innovation in the system of property-taxation: **How Could You Do This?** Among municipalities in the region over 9,000 population, he reports, the law as of 2020 has reduced the per-capita difference in commercial-industrial valuation by slightly more than half; from 13 times to six times. (To see a pdf of the book go to www.centerforpolicy.org/paul-gilje)

The communities 'losing' in the sharing remain the wealthiest. As development patterns change, losers can turn into winners. The program has made the taxes on an average-value house significantly more uniform across the region. Business likes the greater uniformity of the business taxes.

The 'fiscal disparities' (properly, *anti* fiscal disparities') law was much admired but rarely emulated. The Minnesota Legislature later set up a similar program for the Iron Range. And something resembling it was created for the Hackensack Meadowlands in New Jersey. But it was beyond either the political capability or the imagination of most states for their urban regions.

Finding a source of revenue for transit

In enacting the metropolitan sewerage program in 1969 the Legislature set up arrangements for financing its construction and operation. One other operating system, however, still needed financing: transit. The League's involvement with this produced another ingenious 'how'.

After it bought Twin Cities Lines (see Chapter 7) the MTC had begun to build up the bus operation with a combination of fares and a $1-per-vehicle tax in the metropolitan area. Federal aid was part of the answer, but clearly any significant expansion of the system would require some more substantial local revenue.

There was some interest in a gas tax, but the road-user interests always insisted that gas—and vehicle—taxes were for roads only, not for transit. And with property taxes being reduced, that source seemed not available. *What* source, then? And how secured?

Coming to the 1971 session, looking at road finance, Clarence Shallbetter on the League staff noticed how far state gas-tax aid fell short of the total spent for the county road system. The difference, he found, were the county road and bridge levies. He thought: What if the Legislature were to enact a wheelage tax *for county roads*, freeing the road and bridge levies (property-tax revenue) for transit?

This was politically attractive. The wheelage tax is a user tax: The highway lobby could hardly object on principle to a user tax for roads. Then move the former road and bridge levies to transit. Set the levels right and you could get a net property tax reduction in the process.

Martin Sabo, House Speaker, liked the idea. And it passed. Puzzled, the road-user lobby saw transit getting financed and a wheelage tax being added, but had no principle on which to object. Later some of the counties dropped the wheelage tax; went back to levying for county roads. But the tax for transit remained.

So transit got its money. In later years, sales-tax revenue was also provided.

CHAPTER 10:

Re-equalizing School Finance

Minnesota had first enacted an equalization program for public education in the 1950s. Its essential idea was for districts to pay a uniform proportion of their wealth toward the cost of educating the children of their community and, whatever that rate raised in dollars—that amount varying with the differences in property wealth—for the state to pay the balance up to a per-pupil amount deemed adequate (the 'foundation base').

Over the years the Legislature had failed to keep the foundation base up with the rise in actual spending. By the mid-1960s the state was equalizing only up to about half the actual cost per pupil.

In the late 1960s this came to crisis. In addition to the equity problem, the spending for schools was driving effective property-tax rates painfully high. Voters were increasingly rejecting excess-levy referenda and proposals to borrow for capital needs. Aid provided when the sales tax was introduced in 1967 lightened the pressure on property taxes but did not stop the rise in spending. So a crisis was developing as Minnesota came toward 1970 and the gubernatorial election.

Partly the question was 'adequacy'; whether the schools had enough. Partly it was about equity; about citizens in high-value communities being able to finance a rich level of program with relatively low tax rates while citizens in low-value districts paid taxes at a high rate to produce a lower level of program. The Citizens League comparison of taxes on an average-value house (then, $18,000!) showed the disparities; Edina vs. Centennial. School finance was a growing issue nationally. Soon California had the *Serrano* case; Texas the *Rodriguez* decision.

Van Mueller and Jerry Christenson were actively developing the question in Minnesota; Van at the Twin Cities K-12 'service unit' and Jerry as state planning director. The League took the question under study in a committee chaired by Bill Hempel. Its recommendation in June 1970 for a re-equalization—heavily charged politically, with the election coming on—took three meetings to clear the board.

The recommendation was central at the League's annual meeting October 1 when a panel of League actives, John Mooty moderating, questioned the candidates for governor; Douglas Head, the Republican, and Wendell Anderson, the DFLer. Both had left off campaigning for almost a week, getting briefed on League proposals by League actives from their respective parties.

The evening of serious and substantive policy debate would hardly be believed today. I remember David Lebedoff, one of Anderson's advisers, passing by afterward, saying, "Only in Minnesota..." Anderson endorsed—actually, went beyond—the League proposal on K-12 finance. Afterward the Republicans caucused; decided to oppose his plan on grounds it would require a big increase in taxes. As the controversy exploded the DFLers said: Back us; we're supporting your proposal. Mooty advised the staff: Let the report speak for itself.

Anderson was elected. Some years later, when Wendell recalled his unhappiness at not being supported, I reminded him that people in politics were always telling 'good government' groups: 'Be realistic: We can't put ideas ahead of electoral needs and personal loyalties'. I said, "People in politics need to be realistic, too. Those of us working with ideas can't be taking sides in a political fight." Republicans were unhappy with the League as well. I think Doug Head never spoke to me again. But it was hardly the League's fault that a political candidacy misjudged a major question of social equity.

'The Miracle in Minnesota'

The 1971 legislative session did better. It still had a Conservative majority. The majority leader, Stan Holmquist, asked Senator Wayne Popham, with whom the League had worked closely, to take the lead on their response. The regular session ran out. The first special session that enacted 'fiscal disparities' ended without agreement on school finance. Discussions went on privately among legislators until Fall when negotiations at the governor's residence finally produced agreement. A second special session enacted the re-equalization; for the first time, major education finance questions handled not in the education committee but in the tax committee as part of an omnibus finance bill.

It provided for a one-quarter increase in the state income tax and a one-third increase in the sales tax. It was the only case in America of equalization being accomplished through the political process rather than through the courts. A federal judge tried, but was late with his decision: By the time *Van Dusartz* came down legislative action was committed, virtually completed.

The League's school-finance report had recommended adding a 40 per cent weighting for students from AFDC families. That was adopted—as was its recommendation to prohibit local sales and income taxes. A new aid formula for cities was adopted, worked out with legislators by Dean Lund at the League of Cities. Essentially, the Legislature accepted responsibility for the level of local property taxes. It was far-reaching legislation; bipartisan—and controversial: The comment from a fiscal consultant that the package was "largely the work of the Citizens League" was probably not meant as a compliment.

Learning about the legislation, the Advisory Commission on Inter-governmental Relations (ACIR) in 1972 wrote about "The Miracle in Minnesota"—by which John Shannon meant the whole package of fiscal reforms. (Minnesota superintendents continue to appropriate the 'Miracle' term as if the legislative action had been entirely about school finance.)

The schools had gotten a big raise; riding in, as Allan Odden at the Education Commission of the States put it, "on the back of the property-tax revolt". But this was to be the last time the Legislature was to address the problems of public education purely as a matter of money. After 1971 education policy moved to questions about system structure and about learning. Which is another story.

Municipal finance and property-tax relief

John Shannon's work at the ACIR had done much to introduce new ideas into local finance. A 'circuit-breaker' for low-income households. Credits for renters. New forms of state aid. People talked a lot about central cities that were property-rich but, as they came to say, 'overburdened' with poverty-related expenditures.

What developed was a sense of the state at a huge control board, manipulating the switches and dials to make the tax-and-finance system run. Senator McCutcheon, chair of the Senate Tax Committee, saw the state controlling the level of the property tax by the level of local aid it was providing. We asked the chair of the House Tax Committee what he thought was right in terms of taxes paid as a proportion of actual market value. "About one and a quarter percent", he said.

Paul Gilje did superb work with the committees involved in these public-finance issues. He also found Allan Boyce. A junior person working for the Burlington Northern, Allan had impressed Paul with work on a transportation committee. Paul got him to chair a committee on taxes. The subsequent legislative session became in a way a debate between Boyce and John Haynes, Governor Anderson's tax expert. At one hearing in Room 15 Boyce was explaining the essentials of the property tax. With the levy you peg the collections so the rate floats as the base of valuation changes. It's the opposite with non-property taxes, where you peg the rate and float the collections. When he finished, the room, filled largely with assessors, applauded. Word went back to the company about Allan and, as I recall, by the time the railroad moved to Seattle he was an assistant to the president.

When Paul resigned from the League in 1988 there was a heartfelt dinner to recognize his contributions. And, in a way, the League's. I framed and gave him that evening a cartoon from the New Yorker. Down beside a river a beaver is talking to a rabbit. Towering behind them is an enormous concrete dam. "I didn't actually build it", the beaver is saying, "but it was based on my idea."

SECTION FOUR:

TRANSITION IN THE 1970s

The 1970s was a strange decade. Elvis, double-knits and bad hair; Viet Nam and Watergate. It saw huge changes in society, driven partly by the postwar baby-boom generation coming of age. Yet despite—or perhaps because of—the dislocations it was a remarkably productive decade in public affairs; a huge transition as the system adapted to new problems, new ideas, new voices.

It was clear by the end of the 1960s there had been a dramatic crash of confidence in public institutions. Around 1900 the Socialists in Europe and the Progressives in America had turned to government—to public ownership and regulation—to correct the abuses evident in the private sector. Now their idea of 'social control' was being called into question—as the sense grew that government had been captured by the interests it had set out to control or had become itself one of 'the interests'. Some of this critique came from conservatives; the more interesting was coming from the political left.

In Minnesota we saw a winding-up of the work on the institutions for policy-making and financing. We crossed a watershed into a period when the problems were on the operating side of the public sector.

The Citizens League got into this new discussion early in the decade. The 1972 report on contracting led us into a joint project with the Upper Midwest Council on 'public service options', opening a line of policy work that continues today as 'public sector redesign'.

First, though, in Chapter 11, I need to finish the story of Minnesota's work on the 'deciding' side of the public sector: about proposals for the emerging metropolitan structure, for Minneapolis city government and for the Legislature. Chapter 12 winds up a few other initiatives.

Then we'll turn to the new ideas changing everyone's thinking; explain what we were reading and the new voices we were beginning to hear and respond to. This laid the foundation for my later work outside the Citizens League.

CHAPTER 11:

Closing the 'Deciding' Agenda

After the legislative action on the sewerage problem in 1969 the question was whether to set up other regional operations on the same 'service commission' model. Transit and airports were being handled by existing commissions; more (in the case of the MTC) or less (in the case of the MAC) under Metro Council control. Parks and open space was next on the agenda. After that, other public services.

The League had made a successful proposal in 1969 for a new way to modernize the schedule of legislative work. And there was again the old question of 'charter reform'—how to structure Minneapolis city government. Let's take these in order.

Finishing the work on metropolitan affairs

There had been significant national interest in Minnesota's approach to governing the metropolitan region. The ACIR gave it a good deal of attention. So did Dave Durenberger, in the early '80s chairing the U.S. Senate Subcommittee on Intergovernmental Relations. Georgia's legislature copied it for the Atlanta Regional Council. The National

Municipal League gave the Twin Cities area its All-America City award; the first ever to a regional city.

But 'metropolitan' also had its enemies; increasingly, the counties. Also, as Dave Walker at the ACIR said in one of the best talks ever given on the subject, "the vertical autocracies". Anything strengthening general policy-making at any level challenges the power groups working to connect program interests from the national level through to the state to the local level.

Discussion continued about a 'national urban policy'. It rested partly on the notion that a problem occurring everywhere in America needed to be dealt with by the national government. A well-known mayor testifying to Durenberger's subcommittee had no concept whatever of a problem being solved nationwide by action of states and regions, or any sense of Washington's inability constitutionally to change systems existing in state law. It seemed important to explain this. Flying home from the White House Conference on Urban Problems in January 1978 I sketched out a memo: "Federal Policy as the Activation of State Lawmaking".

By the late '70s several pressures were beginning to constrain Minnesota's approach to metropolitan organization. Bernie Hillenbrand at the National Association of Counties sent a senior person, Jim Shipman, here to head their Minnesota association. Shipman organized the effort to ensure the major parks remained largely county parks. Later in the decade the Metro Council tried for a regional solid waste disposal program and for a regional emergency medical system. Neither succeeded.

Internationally there was similar resistance to metropolitan solutions. In Britain, royal commissions chaired by Lord Maud had secured a metropolitan arrangement for London and other big 'conurbations'. Mrs. Thatcher soon destroyed the Greater London Council. France let Paris have a mayor, but the City of Paris is a small part of its urban region. The king never wants the capital city to organize politically.

Elsewhere in America there was little effort at even the Twin Cities area model of regional government—despite the number of regions where action by a single state legislature could have been effective.

Where a region spread into two or more states—as, the New York region—there was no imagination at all. When New York City went into financial crisis—New Jersey and Connecticut next-door having for years run a tax policy aimed at ripping off the city—a regional solution was not discussed.

Conclusions overall re: the Metro Council

So in the end the Star editorial from 1967, "Two Cheers for the Metropolitan Council", proved out. The council was worth having. But the failure to gets its members directly elected proved decisive. In the '80s gubernatorial appointment led to the Metro Council becoming essentially a state agency.

Jerry Isaacs, appointed by Governor Perpich to chair the Council, made an inept effort to take over the regional commissions. Chuck Whiting's editorials in the Tribune scotched that, and Isaacs departed. A search committee proposed Verne Johnson to succeed him. Without even interviewing Verne, Perpich appointed Sandra Gardebring, earlier head of the Pollution Control Agency. In a discussion soon after, about the Council's role in policymaking, Gardebring said simply: "I'm a regulator." From then on the Council did pretty much only what a governor wanted.

The failure was partly self-inflicted. The Council had trouble finding ways to be effective.

Standard planning theory was that from an initial agreement on goals, agreement on policies, programs and projects would logically unfold. Planners' goals, however, tended not to deal with real issues; 'issues' necessarily involving choices. Dave Graven, when a Council member, advised the staff repeatedly: Test the opposite; that will show whether you have a real issue. If your goal is to "Consider environmental effects when designing freeways", try saying, "Do *not* consider environmental effects". If that sounds absurd, you aren't dealing with a real issue.

Planners obsessed about systems being 'fragmented'; assumed that to be coordinated a system had to be under central control. This caused them always to be proposing new regional public utilities. For refuse collection and disposal, for example, they kept advocating 'flow control'—an arrangement that would have required haulers to take their loads to the new burner plants. Our region was saved from this largely by a federal judge who took seriously the laws against monopoly. (Was saved *for a time*. In 2017 the counties are implementing 'flow control', securing the 'organized collection' that completes the transformation of the refuse system into a cost-pass-through arrangement.)

Planners had forever yearned for control, and tended to think of this in terms of final approval on plans proposed by the operating entities, worrying excessively about the details. They did not generalize the strategy that worked with Hennepin County Medical Center (see Chapter 12), which was to set out in advance the things of truly regional interest that were to be done and not to be done, letting the implementing agency know clearly what would be approved and not-approved. The exception was probably the land-planning program led by Bob Hoffman while a member of the Council, to minimize 'urban sprawl'. The Council used its authority over the subordinate Waste Control Commission to tell the municipalities what sewerage capacity would be provided where and at what date; got the cities to relate their individual plans, development programs and zoning to that.

The system of 'subordinate commissions' enacted in 1969 permitted the Council to attend to a variety of major regional questions—including the question of a second airport. In 1994 the Legislature shifted the regional arrangement to the 'operating' model; moving the sewerage and transit responsibilities directly into the Council. (The airports commission, too powerful, was excluded.) Not long after that the Council's administrator, Jim Solem, said he was spending a third or more of his time settling bus drivers' grievances.

By 2010 the issues had significantly changed. Counties, especially, had continued to enlarge their role; handling the regional parks and the solid waste program and creating 'rail authorities' to plan and finance light-rail lines (given to the Council to operate). The counties also worked to get people with local-government background appointed by the governor; in 2016 bringing in a bill to implement essentially the 'council of governments' arrangement. The Citizens League took this under study; proposed an alternative that blocked the county move. Unhappily, the League did not return to its own proposal for direct election.

So the questions both about regional operations and about Council structure and representation remain up in the air; in controversy. Also questions about its policies: A prominent local conservative policy group, the Center of the American Experiment, has been taking after the Council as an unaccountable, out-of-control entity imposing high-density housing and rail-and-bicycle transportation on a population that has not voted for that way of life.

Nevertheless: The Twin Cities area—with its regional council, with the work of the Municipal Commission on annexation and incorporation and with the tax-base-sharing program—has developed better, institutionally and physically, than most metropolitan areas. We will never know how many potential problems have been avoided by the great work the Minnesota Legislature did with the redesign of the regional systems for governmental organization and finance.

City government organization in Minneapolis

Proposals for a strong-mayor form having been voted down in 1948, 1960 and 1963, some re-thinking about 'charter reform' was in order. The 1965 election had brought in a more activist City Council, but decisions about big issues like freeways and transportation were still proving difficult.

Two League committees, both chaired by Jim Weaver, tried to find a workable 'how' for citywide leadership and for securing neighborhood consent.

The logical leader was the mayor. The City Council's desire not to lose control of the departments blocked the idea of making the mayor the executive in a separated-powers system. But might the mayor be given a real leadership role within the strong-council arrangement, on something like the suburban municipal arrangement? In 1969, in "Who

Will Help Us Get Action?" the League suggested putting the mayor in charge of planning and budgeting and—to end their historic rivalry in leadership—merging the offices of mayor and council president.

The planning-and-budgeting was largely accomplished during Al Hofstede's and Don Fraser's time as mayor. We wondered what might happen were Fraser, running for a final term, to get support from Alice Rainville, the council president, for a charter amendment merging the two offices—by offering to resign midway through his term and allowing her to succeed to the new combined leadership office. That did not happen, and Minneapolis has gone on with its curiously mixed system.

Equally pressing was the need for some way to assemble a reasonably effective consensus at a neighborhood level for project issues needing to be decided at that level. Advantaged neighborhoods, like Southeast with its university constituency, had strong and active associations. The Model Cities program in 1965 produced a local council in south Minneapolis. So did the Pilot City program on the north side. "Sub-Urbs in the City" in April 1970 proposed a standard citywide structure.

Members of the City Council were not enthusiastic: "I can just see the chairman of that council running against me at the next election", one alderman said. But such a structure did appear—notably in Saint Paul, which at the time elected its city council members at-large. Fraser, then Minneapolis' congressman, wrote the idea into the local government reorganization for the District of Columbia.

The difficulty in securing local consent was a problem everywhere, because in approving highway or other projects city councils were too often not delivering approvals politically effective in the neighborhoods affected. I might have said something about the 'sub-urbs' idea at the Mount Pocono meeting on transportation planning. I have a letter dated August 1970 from Garland Marple, director of planning for the federal Bureau of Public Roads, saying the suggestion "has provoked considerable discussion in this office" and asking for several more copies. (When Marple retired he sent a note saying he'd appreciated our relationship and that he'd passed his 'Kolderie file' on to his successor Lee Mertz. This helped me see that in Washington officials were hungry for independent, reliable intelligence about local situations. Those handling domestic programs have nothing like the foreign service officers serving the Department of State; they hear only from interested parties wanting, or not-wanting, some particular project. This remains a fundamental problem for the national government when it tries to act on domestic systems. See Chapter 5)

Over the years Minneapolis dwindled; the City Council being quite willing to turn over city functions to Hennepin County. What the Council wants most is to control whatever functions remain with the city. It is forever trying to get control of the park system away from the independently-elected Board of Park Commissioners. And forever failing.*

Legislative reorganization

Minnesota has a strong legislature. This state escaped the initiative and referendum movements in states to the east and west. Until the 1970s its Legislature was nonpartisan. Its Senate is the largest in America.

Early in the '60s I'd begun to hear about Gordon Rosenmeier, a lawyer in Little Falls. The power in the Senate, people said. I asked if we might talk. Meet me at the Minneapolis Club, he said. I nursed one brandy while he drank his Scotch and sodas. And explained Minnesota's government.

Minnesota is a great state. The heart of the state is its government. At the heart of its government is the Legislature. At the heart of the Legislature is the Senate. At the heart of the Senate is the Committee on Civil Administration. Rosenmeier, first elected in 1940, served for years on Civil Administration: He chaired its subcommittee on state departments, which meant he controlled what governors wanted. He chaired

---

* Note as of 2021: Much has now changed; in the politics of the city, in the background of persons elected mayor and in the composition and character of the City Council. Issues about zoning and transportation divide the younger, 'progressive', council members from older residents. And the council's initial impulse to 'defund the police' after the killing of George Floyd in May 2020 has been countered by the desire for police protection by north Minneapolis neighborhoods plagued by gun violence. The Charter Commission has taken the new situation, and the unpopularity of the City Council, as an opportunity to put the 'strong mayor' form of city government up for approval again in the November 2021 election.

the subcommittee of Senate Finance that controlled what the University wanted. He chaired the Judiciary Committee, controlling what the lawyers and the courts wanted. He chaired the Committee on Committees that handled assignments the legislators wanted. Close associates often came to chair committees Rosenmeier did not chair himself. In 1967, with the question of metropolitan government coming up, he chaired the division of Civil Administration handling metropolitan problems.

Reapportionment had followed *Baker v. Carr*, the U.S. Supreme Court decision requiring equal-population-district representation. And in 1973 the DFL had introduced party designation. Staffing had increased. But the Legislature needed a greater capacity to do work. It needed a redesign.

There was only modest interest in cutting its size. Occasionally someone suggests making Minnesota's legislature a unicameral, like Nebraska's (which Nebraskans say is far too small and which, they explain, is a bicameral *functionally*). Size matters, in a representative system. In Minnesota you can still reasonably expect to find a candidate for the state House of Representatives at your door asking for your vote.

Nor was there any great call here for annual full-year sessions. California's Assembly Speaker, Jesse Unruh, was pushing this, as was the National Conference of State Legislatures he'd helped form. But that big-state model seemed excessive. Nor was there interest in North Dakota's Legislative Research Committee; a kind of executive committee that between sessions worked through the major issues and prepared the major bills.

There *was* broad agreement that Minnesota's Legislature needed somewhat more time and a different schedule. As always, the key was the 'how'. In 1968 a League committee chaired by Peter Seed had come up with idea of a 'flexible session': 120 legislative days divided between the first five months of each year of the biennium. The Legislature put this proposed constitutional amendment to the voters in the fall of 1972 and voters approved. (See page 64.)

In some ways the modernized legislature is better. The state does a two-year budget in the odd year. Bills are now publicly available when introduced. The old seniority system has disappeared. Minnesota has not gone to term limits.

But the influence of the individual legislator has declined. The professional staff, which discourages radical policy change, has grown in size and become more dominant. Here as elsewhere, too, legislators are now caught in the public's sharper partisanship.

The legislative process suffers today partly from the weakening or disappearance of the groups that in earlier years brought to it public-interest analyses of the state's needs and opportunities, and proposals for redesign. And that did so much to broaden legislators' thinking. Work on population-change and its implications usefully survives in an office inside the Department of Administration, but state planning, with its 'Horizons' briefings, is virtually gone. We will come back to this problem in Section Seven.

CHAPTER 12:

Housing, Sports, Public Television, Hospitals

Before discussing the transition I want to cover a few matters in which the League played a minor part; and a few questions it thought about but did not actively engage. Only one was truly governmental. Others involved what the League called 'quasi-public' facilities or systems; non-governmental but with a public dimension to them.

Housing

The League was not active in the construction/development issues; was not in the debate about what housing was to be built where. Or, for example, in the effort to reduce the price of housing: There were enough voices in that discussion.

Early in the 1970s, at a drug store in Washington, I ran into Anthony Downs, a classmate at Carleton. Quickly we discovered we were both now in urban policy. Tony saw the essentials of big issues, housing especially, more clearly than anyone.

Zoning ordinances and building codes make it illegal to build new low-cost (i.e., small-unit, cheap-to-build) housing. This meant that low-cost housing—inexpensive, so it can be priced for the poor—could be produced only by converting existing buildings. This was what confined people of low-income to the central cities where the region's stock of old buildings existed. In the developing suburbs new housing had to be high-cost construction, so was not available to the poor.

Tony had a major hand, along with Victor Palmieri, in the Kerner Commission report. But despite that, and earlier work with an unpublicized task force for President Johnson, no solution for this problem emerged. One compromise was to build costly units and reduce their price with subsidy. But the efforts to get subsidized housing into the suburbs with Section 8 vouchers was small, and resisted. Time, of course, will help to some degree: As the small early-post-war suburban housing ages it will become more attractive to the poor—while perhaps the central cities build new.

The League did arrange some discussions about a utilization strategy. It seemed an appealing idea to focus more of the new construction on smaller units for older couples and single persons, freeing up existing houses for the new families just being formed. It was a 'utilization' strategy, of limited appeal to a producer-dominated system, so got no real attention as a strategy.

I had always had in the back of my mind, too, the unitization I'd seen in the North Dakota oil industry. Assembling tracts large enough for redevelopment was hard for a private developer. Condemnation by public authority was resisted, existing owners not wanting to be forced out so some developer could make a killing. The unitization idea was that if some defined proportion of the land could be assembled, the holdout parcels would be required to join the unit; not bought out, but given a stake in the success of the new development.

Issues in the housing system continue to need good thinking. Minneapolis and Saint Paul are rapidly changing. New apartments and condos are being constructed, as I write, with warehouses—and especially in Saint Paul, older office buildings—being converted into 'lofts'. In Saint Paul owners of low-cost housing went to court to stop the city from using its housing codes to force improvements; arguing this violated federal law by producing a 'disparate impact' on the poor. The trial court ruled for the city but the appellate court reversed that decision. The case was about to be heard in the U.S. Supreme Court when Mayor Chris Coleman was persuaded to drop the city's appeal.

The stadium

Planning and siting facilities for the area's major-league sports was the kind of question the League thought ideal for the Metropolitan Council. But when the question of a new stadium for the Twins and Vikings appeared, the governor claimed the lead role. Perpich put Peter Vanderpoel, now his state planning director, in charge.

Various of us talked with Joe Robbie, evenings in his law office. Joe had by that time become managing partner of the Miami Dolphins, so knew all the major questions: single-purpose or dual-purpose, domed or open-air, televised or blacked-out.

A big question was: On which side of downtown should the Metrodome be located? Tommy Thompson, Minneapolis city coordinator, wanted it on the west side, integrated with the big parking ramps. The university apparently wanted it on the east side, closer to campus. Some of us went to explain the controversy to John Cowles Jr., the Star and Tribune being a leading backer for the stadium. Why didn't somebody tell me all this before? The ultimate outcome was east of downtown, dual-purpose, domed, carpet-on-concrete.

Gradually the region's quasi-public facilities, arts and sports, have been evolving from multi-purpose to single-purpose. The Twins got their own new stadium in 2010; open-air; west of the downtown; finally, what Tommy Thompson had wanted. The university got a new stadium on campus; pulled its football out of the Metrodome. Pro football stayed in the Metrodome until with Governor Dayton's support there was a deal for a new Vikings stadium. It opened in 2016. Domed. A billion dollars.

The League did one study on youth sports, with a staffer—Brad Richards—who'd been all-state in two sports at Minneapolis Southwest.

Later he was a hockey recruiter for Princeton, so knew the Canadian system; youth sports community-based rather than school-based. The report talked about moving to that model. The High School League was not amused.

Public television and 'The Bottom Line'

The Twin Cities area was early into 'educational television'. It was, as later the new people would say, more education than television: sometimes a person with a pointer standing by a map, talking. The League was urged to program a look at changing to modern 'public' television: the BBC, PBS, WGBH and all that. We did, and recommended that change. Quickly that happened; driven surely by contributors.

The new management under Bill Kobin proposed an evening strip of local programming: Monday Joleen Benoit's entertainment show; Tuesday and Thursday Gary Gilson's magazine; Wednesday Jim Klobuchar on sports and a Friday evening public affairs show initially called The Bottom Line, a journalists' discussion modeled on and leading into the PBS Washington Week in Review. When a local newspaperman proved uncomfortable on camera, KTCA asked me to try out. That seemed to work, and I got away for seven years as the on- and off-camera editor of a serious public affairs program on a VHF channel in a major market in prime time. Gradually the earlier shows in the strip went out and only our Friday public affairs show remained.

In time the station's producers wanted something livelier and more visual; more appealing to a younger demographic. My show was replaced by Almanac; what Kobin described to me just before he left as "a pop show". It still runs; a long success; good people whom I like and respect.

We did pretty well, though; both when it was The Bottom Line and later when it shifted to journalists interviewing some public figure. The ratings, I heard, were good. But real television people, I knew, were grumbling in the dark corners of the studio that it was "a radio show with pictures". Too serious. Television, I came to understand, is about compelling pictures and emotion. Floods and fires; tears and triumph.

Once in a while I meet people who say they remember that show. I ask: "How old were you then?" I love it when they say, "twenty-five".

Hennepin County General Hospital

The League had come into the hospital issues through its support in 1963 of the transfer of Minneapolis General Hospital to Hennepin County. 'General' had long been important for emergency care and for medical training. But the spread of insurance that gave people free choice of hospital, ending the dual system of care, was about to deprive General of its base of indigent patients.

As expected, the county quickly proposed to build a new facility. It won voter approval for a bond issue—that was, however, absurdly small. As commissioners saw the need for a second round of financing the county came to the League again for support. At a meeting one afternoon we asked that they commit to get the approval of the Metropolitan Health Board before building. They agreed. We suggested they put that in writing, and the board did pass a resolution.

The League then went to Jim Hetland, chair of the Metropolitan Council and said: The planning will take two years, will cost big money and will produce a stack of paper a foot high. If the Health Board waits until the plan comes in it'll be impossible to change anything. You need to say ahead of time what you want the county to do and not to do.

The Health Board created a task force to develop guidelines for the Hennepin County planning. What emerged was simple and clear: a maximum dollar cost, so many square feet, a maximum number of beds and, most significant, a requirement to be "co-located and contiguous" with the private Metropolitan Medical Center (MMC) a block away— defined as a wall-to-wall multi-story interface. Come in with this and the project will be approved; come in with something else and it will not.

A move by the region's hospital administrators to divert the question into a 'technical committee' of administrators was rebuffed. The critical meeting took place at the Capp Towers motel one Saturday morning. Representatives from the hospitals found the task force firm. Give us

the weekend, they said. They and their architects went off for a char-
rette; came back Monday saying they could do it. The county moved its
proposed building site a block east. Today you can see the multi-story
'linking facility' over Chicago Avenue. In time MMC was absorbed into
Hennepin County Medical Center.

It was a fascinating lesson in the 'how' of planning. Too many planners too often assumed that generalized 'goals and policies' up front and
a requirement for 'final approval' would
provide effective direction to and control
of the implementing agencies. They
waited until the plan came in, then fussed
with its details. (Ray Haik remembers the
Metropolitan Council planners arguing
once with the Nine Mile Creek watershed
district whether its ponding area should be marsh or open water.)

*Establish the few
key things that truly
matter and give the big
agencies fair warning*

The way to be effective is to establish the few key things that
truly matter and give the big agencies, early and clearly, fair warning
that approval depends on their complying with these major regional
concerns.

The redesign of the region's hospital system

The question involving General Hospital was part of a larger question about the future of the regional hospital system, which went into
a re-structuring during the 1970s. The size of the hospital plant was in
turn part of the larger problem of cost in this huge and growing non-
governmental 'public' system.

Anne and Herman Somers caught perfectly that problem of cost,
and its cause, in **Medicare and the Hospitals** in 1976: *"In no other realm
of economic life is repayment guaranteed for costs that are neither controlled
by competition nor regulated by public authority and in which no incentive for
economy can be discerned."*

Victor Cohn had begun writing about the system problem at the
Tribune in the 1950s. Historically, people paid their doctor and hospital

bills privately—if they could. Those who couldn't went to the public hospital for 'indigent care'. But as the idea of 'prepayment' appeared, and evolved into 'hospital insurance', the system of financing changed. Hospitals could build-in a charge for capital; then borrow against this stream of funds to finance their building program. As this method for financing construction grew, the private hospital fund drives disappeared. Hospitals had direct access to the money needed to upgrade or expand.

The region's hospitals had been concentrated in central Minneapolis and Saint Paul. They wanted to rebuild. At the same time, new suburbs wanted their own hospitals. The prospect of an oversupply of beds produced a program of hospital planning, here as around the country. Voluntary at first, its reviews soon came to be required for approval to build: Minnesota enacted a 'certificate of need' requirement in 1971. The Metropolitan Health Board under the Metropolitan Council inherited the tough question: Would the region both upgrade its existing city hospitals *and* build new hospitals in the suburbs?

Vic Cohn had become interested in Kaiser-Permanente in California and in pre-paid care. So had Paul Ellwood at InterStudy, who began to promote the idea here. As this developed and spread in the Twin Cities area the length of stay in hospitals began to fall. An actuary for Prudential, Harry Sutton, remembered that when he left for the Newark home office in the 1970s the area was running about 1,200 patient days per thousand in general acute care. When he returned a decade later that was down to about 400 days per thousand. That drop in demand complicated the decision about construction; about new and replacement beds.

The Citizens League played some part in the redesign of the hospital plant that took place. In 1976 a study committee compared the Twin Cities area with Seattle-Tacoma; found the two regions almost identical in size and in demographic and socio-economic makeup. But Seattle-Tacoma, with its more politically constrained method of financing construction, had a hospital system about half the size of ours. And no difference in health status between the two regions could be seen. Hospital executives, disturbed, tested the comparison with Seattle-Tacoma but could not shake it.

The League recommended taking out up to 3,000 beds. It was a startling recommendation at a time when some surveys still thought that having *more* beds per capita helped define 'the best cities' in America.

We forced the question: How can the hospital system justify carrying so many more beds than necessary, sending the costs through the insurance system to the community for payment? The League recommended a hospital trustees' council be formed to deal with the question.

Fritz Corrigan, chair of the Abbott-Northwestern board, called to ask me to come and explain. I did. Soon after, we heard, he invited the other chairs of the Minneapolis area hospital boards to lunch at the Minikhada Club. The hospitals' executives were not invited. A trustees' council did then form. The strategy was first to group the hospitals into larger organizations; then to reduce bed-capacity within each larger merged institution.

A key remaining question was University Hospitals. Earlier the general hospital for the state (outside Minneapolis and Saint Paul), it too had lost its role in indigent care. As Ellwood pointed out, this left it a tertiary-care and teaching hospital with no base of primary-care patients; so probably not viable. The university proposed a big expansion anyway; sold that to the Legislature. Immediately after getting approval the three university health-care executives involved left the state. In time Fairview, a largely primary-care hospital group, took over University Hospitals, confirming Ellwood's analysis.

The hospital controversy offered several lessons. The debate underlined again how important it was to have a sophisticated understanding and discussion about the way a system works and to have knowledgeable reporting about its problems: Gordon Slovut at the Star and Lewis Cope at the Tribune were following this discussion closely. And how important it was to have had generalist trustees, rather than only the professional administrators, involved. (We had seen earlier the importance of having the elected mayors rather than just city managers involved in the debate about metropolitan organization.)

"You're not wrong because people disagree with you"

Finally, after the intense controversy, the outcome was a welcome reminder that you're not wrong because people disagree with you.

• • •

A new agenda for policy in the '70s

Through the 1960s, as it seemed so many of the old practices were being challenged, various institutions began responding. The business community created an Urban Coalition and stayed with it longer than did business in other cities. Russ Ewald moved in down the hall from us with the Equal Opportunities Fund. Fairly quickly after the brief period in which a former police chief, Charlie Stenvig, was mayor in Minneapolis, politics righted itself; Al Hofstede succeeding Stenvig.

In 1972 the DFL party won full control of state government for the first time in Minnesota history. The 1970s then proved a decade of significant accomplishment.

Minnesota's work brought it serious national attention. Gurney Breckenfeld from Fortune came here to look at urban development. John Fischer, the editor of Harpers, wrote up the 'governance' changes. Neal Peirce came, updating his series on The States of America. Governor Anderson was on the cover of TIME.

Looking at what had been done, the outsiders were increasingly curious: *How* was this done? That got some—like the Kettering Foundation—curious about the Citizens League. We said that if they'd all come here together, we'd explain. In April 1976 they did. We wrote up the results as "The Citizens League Itself", which circulated widely.

Minnesota basked in this glow. In 1980 when Bob Holland of the Committee for Economic Development asked what challenges Minnesotans saw coming next, those at the Spring Hill meeting could not think of any. Outside, afterward, Harlan Cleveland, then newly-arrived, said: "Any community that thinks it can just sit on its accomplishments is in for a shock in the last quarter of the 20th century".

That proved prophetic. Some major changes were making themselves evident; beginning to set quite a different agenda for our public affairs.

SECTION FIVE:

OPENING THE 'DOING' AGENDA

In the 1970s challenges began to appear to the traditional assumptions about the way things are done in the public sector. Everett Carll Ladd documented the crash of public confidence in institutions, private and governmental. He found the public maintaining its support for the high-service state—but clearly wanting it more effectively and economically run.

That made it seem efforts to cut back the social role of government were unlikely to prevail—and that efforts to extend entitlements and expand services should be accompanied by a commitment to find more effective and responsive ways to carry out what the public wanted done.

Clearly this had huge political implications; suggested a coming-together around the idea of the high-service state using new and different approaches for the implementation of policies and the delivery of programs.

Our work came to focus on the alternatives possible. Some of it was conceptual work. Some of it was design work. Some of it was test-and-demonstrations. Some of it was implementation. A lot got done. As the '80s proceeded, this work—initially applied only to general local government—transitioned into public education: We will pick up that story in Section Six. First, I want to capture what we learned about the essential ideas of what we came to call redesign.

Chapter 13 sets the background; mentions some of the ideas we found influential and discusses the League's initial ventures with these new approaches to public action. Chapter 14 describes the work with others interested in 'alternative service delivery'. Chapter 15 sets out the basic concepts and strategies and discusses lessons learned about the 'how' of redesign. Finally, in Chapter 16 I try to explain and describe the 'settings' in which the work of redesign got done; that are necessary for it to get done.

CHAPTER 13:

Reconsidering 'Social Control'

In the 1960s programs earlier regarded as good and necessary came under criticism from all directions. In St. Louis public housing was demolished. Urban renewal (initially, 'slum clearance') was now intensely resisted. So were freeways, increasingly. Long-established institutions and political processes were challenged as unresponsive. There was pressure to reform welfare. There was beginning to be a cry to scale back government.

Looking at his polling data Everett Carll Ladd described the country as "in between idea-systems". **The Age of Discontinuity** Peter Drucker called it.

Clearly the questions went beyond how to organize the policy-making side of the public sector. The challenges now had to do with the scope of policy-making and with the effectiveness, cost and responsiveness of the mechanisms through which policy was trying to act. That got us quickly to the central question: If government is essentially a decider, are there other ways its policy decisions can be carried out? Is government able to make that adjustment itself? If not, how can so important a change be made?

The effort to expand the scope and role of government had begun in the 19th century as theorists and activists never themselves influential began to see the potential for power in leveraging the emerging movement for popular democracy to address the economic and social problems created by industrialization. The English historian E.H. Carr, in his lectures at Cambridge in 1962, saw the new idea as *"the belief in the capacity of man to control his economic destiny by conscious action..."* Aneurin Bevan, the Labour minister creating Britain's National Health Service, said: *"Society must be brought under control in exactly the same way as man has tried to bring natural forces under control."* Establishing that 'control' became the agenda of politics; the role assigned to government.

'The New Nationalism'

In America that broadening concept of government's role—the notion of "the larger community, represented by government" as I once heard a Harvard professor put it—had come into national politics with Theodore Roosevelt.

Eric Goldman described in **Rendezvous With Destiny** the dilemma facing liberal reformers after 1900 and how it was solved; how the way was opened here to 'social control' and to the high-service state. Herbert Croly, a New York journalist, saw the reformers trying to attack the abuses of the industrial system—railroads, oil companies, banks, other large corporations—and failing. Reformers had resisted the idea of a strong central government, seeing it dominated by the rich and powerful. That commitment to small-scale Jeffersonian democracy left them no way to reach the abuses of the business corporations now national in scope.

In 1909 Croly pointed the way out in **The Promise of American Life**, calling for action by *a national government reformed and made democratic so it would act in the interests of the common people*. It was the idea of the Hamiltonian state used for Jeffersonian ends. The person to lead that, Croly wrote, was Theodore Roosevelt.

It was the idea of the Hamiltonian state used for Jeffersonian ends

120

Back from Africa, Roosevelt invited him to Oyster Bay; listened, bought the idea and took it across the country in the summer of 1910 beginning with the speech to the veterans of the Grand Army of the Republic at Osawatomie, Kansas. (He stopped at Saint Paul to talk about 'Conservation', staying at its fine new hotel.) 'The New Nationalism' speech was the "I stand for the square deal" speech; the "I regard the executive as the steward of the public welfare" speech. It became *the* 20th-century American political program: into the public sector, up to the national level, over to the executive branch.

Denied the Republican nomination in 1912, Roosevelt formed the Progressive Party and ran anyway; split the Republican vote with the result that Woodrow Wilson was elected. Wilson offered The New Freedom. In the '30s Franklin Roosevelt had The New Deal, then Harry Truman The Fair Deal, then John Kennedy The New Frontier, then Lyndon Johnson The Great Society. It had been a powerful simple idea. But by the 1960s, growing larger and spinning faster, it was coming apart.

Challenges to the high-service state

"Every reform will in time be carried to an excess which will itself need reforming", somebody said. By 1970 'the New Nationalism' needed reforming. The impulse was still to think of solving public problems as something government did. But the evident problems with implementation were forcing a rethinking. A new idea system needed to appear, about how government would do things and about how institutions could be re-formed.

On a visit to the Humphrey Institute a Harvard neo-conservative, Edward Banfield, pointed out this shift. Defending the earlier agenda, a good Minnesota liberal said essentially: We meant well. What does that matter, Banfield replied: Look what a mess you made. In England Norman Macrae, deputy editor of The Economist, was devastating about "the people we have become".

Political conservatism was on the rise, in America as in Europe. Barry Goldwater fell short in 1964 but four years later a different Republican won and for 40 years after that all the presidents were to be Republicans or moderately centrist Democrats.

The critique from the political right was increasingly effective and successful. The critique from the left was more interesting and perhaps more important.

"Professionalism is one of the great hopes", Professor Levy had said to us at Princeton. Now John McKnight was seeing 'professionalism'—doctors, educators, counselors and social workers, all financed increasingly by government programs—as people in search of an income, denying individuals and families the right to deal with their problems themselves, hiding their private interests behind "I care for you"; behind "The Mask of Love".

By 1970 the feeling was strong that in some respects government had become an 'interest' itself. Anthony Downs had shown in 1957 in **An Economic Theory of Democracy** how public organizations have essentially private interests. Tony Bouza, brought in from New York City to be chief of police, described the Minneapolis department as "a chocolate factory", run for the convenience of the people who worked in it.

Ralf Dahrendorf at the London School of Economics wrote in **Life Chances** in 1979 about "The End of the Social-Democratic Consensus"; nicely summarized in the New Yorker by William Pfaff.

On the night of the British election in 1979 Ed Fogelman invited a few people to his home on Summit Avenue in Saint Paul to listen to the returns with Dick Leonard. Leonard had co-edited **The Socialist Agenda**, essays in memory of Anthony Crosland. In one, "The Place of Public Expenditure in Socialist Thought", the economist Colin Crouch wrote: *"Another way of beating off the challenge from the Right is to ensure that the pattern of public services deserves wholehearted support . . . (But) too often socialists seem unwilling to accept any re-examination, being committed to defend any public spending apart from armaments regardless of whether it continues to serve much useful purpose . . . Take council housing. Envisaged at a time when virtually the only other choice for people was to be the tenant of a private landlord, it now has to be evaluated in a society where most people own their own homes. Council housing is not administered primarily in the interests of the people who live in it, but on behalf of an entirely depersonalized* *'public'; its inhabitants are merely tenants. . . . Tackling the problem is not easy, but much of Labour acts as though there were no problem at all."*

Mrs. Thatcher, elected that night after 'the winter of discontent' in Britain, moved immediately to let people buy the council housing in which they lived.

It was all a serious challenge to beliefs long and deeply held by persons brought up in the New Deal tradition. But gradually beliefs, thinking, positions—and politics—began to change. More and more, people wanted to know *why* organizations behaved as they did, and how problems were to be corrected. They were finding their way to the understanding that problems are the product of circumstances, best dealt with by changing the circumstances that produce them; getting to the heart of problems where, as Monnet wrote, "things are simple'. (See pages 136, 161.)

Problems are the product of circumstances

Paul Ellwood and Walter McClure, working on the medical/hospital problem, pointed to the system-incentives. Walt published an outstanding paper in 1972. There is, to be sure, market failure in this system, he wrote. But the answer to market failure is not regulation, because there is regulatory failure too and regulatory failure is worse because so much harder to correct. The proper response to market failure is market reform. That proved a powerful idea; among other things putting into perspective the nonsense that markets are 'free' markets. A market is a construct; is designed; needs to be designed well.

You could sense the shift in the reaction to the concept of 'social control'. Think about the ambivalence in the term: flood control, crop control, price control; Control Data and Mission Control, 'under control' and 'out of control'. But also: birth control, crowd control, gun control, climate control. What control is good; when is it not good? Who controls? How? In whose interest? Do people want to be 'controlled'?

Yale's Charles Lindblom caught perfectly the essence of the different approaches to coordinated control. When John Bryson brought him to the Humphrey Institute he distinguished between 'mechanisms of central authority' and 'mechanisms of mutual adjustment'. At the smallest scale and at the largest, he said, control is through mutual adjustment; the market mechanism, essentially. Yet the idea of coordination through central authority never fades. *"The influence of people trained to think of the situation in its entirety, with their bias in favor of acting comprehensively, continues to be one of the major intellectual problems in the organization of human action."*

When gathering materials for the leadership program at the Humphrey Institute I'd come across a telling comment by a president of MIT: *"The rate of change, even more than the change itself, is the dominant fact of our time"*. The resulting, dramatic, changes in society generated pressures to broaden social responsibility ... which of course forced more sharply the questions about how that should be done.

In 1976, in his lectures at Harvard, Charles Schultze—director of budget and after that chairman of the Council of Economic Advisers for President Johnson—saw this, and suggested a greater reliance on incentives. *"The economic and social forces that flow from growth and affluence will continue to throw up problems and attitudes that call for intervention of a very complex order"*, he wrote. *"Even were it politically possible—which it is not— we cannot handle the dilemma by abjuring a further extension of interventionist policies. But equally we cannot afford to go on imposing command-and-control solutions over an ever-widening sphere of social and economic activity."* Incentives, he argued, make it possible to act without violating the first rule of political life, which is that 'Thou Shalt Do No Direct Harm'.

Politics were scrambled, as ideas were scrambled. What used to be thought of as 'left' and 'right' now seemed to form a circle: libertarian conservatives and radical community activists allied against the big institutions: governments and corporations. Yet in some cities in the '60s—in Minneapolis—the new and influential neighborhood interest was accepted and supported by the civic and business leadership. Often philanthropy and business allied with the neighborhood activists. Street-front alternative schools appeared. Some firms developed an interest in 'corporate social responsibility'.

In 1973 the Democratic-Farmer-Labor (DFL) party, in full control of state government for the first time, moved to implement the traditional liberal program long blocked by Minnesota's Conservative Senate. It did enact much of that agenda. But the changed situation was soon to lead to some different and important new concepts of the public sector.

Public Service Options

The Citizens League got started early—in a sense got Minnesota started—thinking about the policy response. In 1971, influenced by the discussion in Washington about management by objectives and by the business community interest in 'social responsibility', we looked at contracting. The report "Why Not Buy Service?" appeared early in 1972. That report distinguished between government as decider and government as doer; between 'providing' and 'producing'—an idea with which we were to be deeply involved.

George Thiss approached the League about a joint venture with the Upper Midwest Council to develop the concept and to stimulate some demonstrations in local government. We organized Public Service Options (PSO) with support from the Bush, McKnight and Ford foundations. Much of Minnesota's work on system redesign over the succeeding 40 years has come out of the thinking generated in that project.

The PSO staff worked to get local units to try contract arrangements: to get Hennepin County to consider buying meals for its new medical center rather than building its own food-factory, for example; suggested to Mayor Latimer that Saint Paul contract to handle the (temporary) problem of disposing of dead elm trees.

We began to find that, as there is private-regarding behavior inside government, there can also be public-regarding behavior in private organizations. I saw a young man turned away at the drivers' license bureau because something was wrong with his form. "You'll have to come back tomorrow." He said: "I work; I can't get time off every day. Why can't you be open in the evening?" What could she say? Not long after that I was trying to get home from Milwaukee through the commuter airline system; found it could get me as far as Eau Claire at 10:30. I figured I'd drive from there. I called Hertz. "We close at 10", she said, "but I'll wait for you."

More and more groups were working on strategies for public-sector productivity, using the concepts we were later to call 'redesign'. League committees delved into the medical/hospital system. One did good work on public transit, where a huge debate was under way (See Chapter 7). Another, considering the push for a state university in the metropolitan area, began thinking about a 'college without a campus'. State Rep. Rod Searle read about this in the committee minutes and in the 1971 session (in the conference committee, as I recall) created Metropolitan State University on those principles.

Work began at last on public education: on bargaining, Saint Paul school buildings, the downsizing required in Minneapolis by the end of the Baby Boom, differentiated staffing, accountability, desegregation. It was a new experience for superintendents, seeing their issues come out in public.

After increasing the financing for Minneapolis and Saint Paul in 1971 state legislative leadership found them immediately coming back for more. Why does it cost so much to run these cities? House Speaker Martin Sabo and Nick Coleman, the Senate majority leader, put Tom Fulton and bright young researchers to work on pensions, refuse collection and disposal, other services.

Nationally, interest was growing in 'alternative service delivery': RAND; the Urban Institute, SRI International, the International City Managers Association in its New Horizons project, John McGwire at the National Science Foundation who partnered with the MANC organizations in 1973-74.

PSO ran until 1978; suggesting that government itself need not always be the 'producer' of service and broadening significantly the concept of alternative approaches available. Increasingly we were interested in public bodies having both options; administration and contract. Chuck Neerland went with me to explain the recommendations to Mayor Hofstede, for whom he'd earlier worked in Minneapolis. Al said immediately: "I get it. A smart rat has two holes." (We made it 'gopher' in the final report.) We titled the report "A Better Way"; followed it with an implementation report titled "On the Way".

Increasingly we were interested not only in alternative ways of delivering service but also in alternatives *to* the 'service' model; in *non*-service strategies. We heard more about this on a trip to Denmark in August 1980 (about which more below).

'Issues of the '80s'

As interest and momentum developed it seemed to make sense to cap the decade by building this work into the ongoing program of the Citizens League. The League created a special, select, committee to consider how to continue this redesign effort; the "Issues of the '80s" committee, chaired by Dave Graven. We were able to talk with people working with the ideas most important in this emerging policy area. The board adopted the report, "Enlarging Our Capacity to Adapt", with its view of government as essentially a decider searching for alternative ways of 'doing'.

Implementation would be a challenge. We could feel changes coming in community life; in the civic system. Corporate public affairs was being reoriented to serve the commercial interests of the firm. The region's major business firms were growing, becoming increasingly national; less concerned with the headquarters community. Business was increasingly oriented to Washington. "The insurance industry is the last major industry in this country still to believe in a framework of state regulation as a matter of principle", an executive at The St. Paul Companies said to me in 1980. "And you can't imagine the pressure we're under to change that."

I called on Honeywell about its annual contribution. Don Conley, the public affairs vice president, was happy to renew their contribution. "My problem is Congress", he said—meaning, its growing inclination to make weapons systems decisions politically. I said I'd understood Honeywell did not seek prime contracts. That's true, he said, but it's getting so you won't be considered for the subcontracts if you haven't been involved in lobbying for the prime.

Public-affairs officers asked each other which they would rather fight: 'Fifty chimps or one gorilla'. The correct answer, they decided, was 'one gorilla'. That took me back to Goldman, to **Rendezvous with Destiny**, in which he'd quoted Vernon Parrington's concern in 1929 about Croly's idea for a new Hamiltonian state: *"We must have a political state powerful enough to deal with corporate wealth, but how are we going to keep that state with its augmenting power from being captured by the force we want it to control?"* We were to hear that concern again.

> *The correct answer was 'one gorilla'*

In the '70s the newspapers changed. The coverage of public affairs shifted subtly in its perspective, from 'What *we* are doing in this community' to 'What *they* are doing to *you*'. The growing emphasis on the reader, on 'You', followed from studies showing that what people actually read most were advice columns. Your health. Your job. Your home. Your children. How to invest. Where to vacation. Where to dine.

The law business changed: Advertising removed the need for lawyers to be active in order to be known, and their offices were pushing them to account for billable time. Legislators no longer had an 'off year' between sessions. Staff roles grew as the Legislature professionalized.

A personal transition

Early in '80 it was time to leave the League. Russ Ewald offered me a sabbatical; whether from the McKnight Foundation itself or the Bingers personally I was never quite sure. I said yes. Curt Johnson became executive director. I began to pursue on my own these questions about the redesign of the public sector.

CHAPTER 14:

Separating Doing from Deciding

My 'sabbatical' began that fall. Homer Wadsworth put me on the staff of the Cleveland Foundation. I worked at home; going back over what we'd learned from PSO, aiming to begin with a paper setting out the general framework for what we were calling 'service redesign'; the 'options' strategy.

The work ended up running about a year and a half; the paper appearing as "Many Providers/Many Producers" in April 1982 after I'd joined the Humphrey Institute. I sent copies around town and around the country. In those days busy people read such things: I still have that file of responses; find the number and seriousness of them quite amazing.

I'll set out here only what's helpful for understanding how the 'redesign' ideas began to move during the 1980s. First, we had to clarify these new concepts of policy action; distinguish them from the conventional effort that assumed the bureau model and that assumed management could get the bureau to perform better. Second, we needed to find the 'how' by which those new concepts would be introduced.

I had come to suggest people think in terms of a four-part field of action:

	REVENUE SIDE ACTIONS	EXPENDITURE SIDE ACTIONS
Short-term Actions	TAX	CUT
Long-term actions	GROW	REDESIGN

Three of these were obvious. Everyone knows cutting and taxing; everyone yearns to grow the economy. The challenge was to explore the 'southeast corner' of the policy field; to find what could be done, even if not quickly, that would accomplish public objectives more economically, more effectively and more responsively. Surely there must be some alternative to endlessly raising revenue and cutting program. If so, that approach might promise a gain in productivity for the public sector. There was beginning to be a glimmer of hope that success with the strategy might also hold the potential for a new political alignment.

I drew a graphic to make the point that between the resources going in and the results coming out there is some mechanism that turns resources into results.

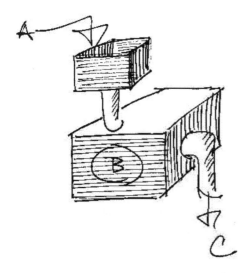

Most people initially thought about the traditional mechanism: A government body hiring employees to do things for people for pay; 'delivering service' through the public bureau model. The public body owns and runs the operation; is both decider and doer, provider and producer.

So long as only that historic mechanism was inside the box the response in every fiscal crisis was the standard "Folks, there are only two choices." Tax or cut. "If you want more out, you have to put more in. If you put less in, you will get less out."

Yet it was clear that government *does* have other ways to carry out its policy objectives. Subsidy, regulation, contracting are ways of 'doing things' that involve doers that are not the public bureau. So we began with alternatives already in use.

Moving to the Humphrey Institute

Harlan Cleveland had come to be dean at what was then the Hubert H. Humphrey Institute of Public Affairs. He wanted to collect some 'reflective practitioners', to be 'senior fellows' (a title not then in use at this university). I was one of these.

High on his agenda was to develop a new program in 'reflective leadership'. Harlan was interested in 'governance beyond government'; had a sense himself of the country being between idea systems. Through that first year he brought in old friends and acquaintances. One was James Callaghan, Britain's former prime minister who had known Humphrey. In a small morning discussion about the concept of leadership Callaghan talked about those who have a vision of the future; Weizman, for example, with Zionism. Then he said: "I don't think anybody was ever better than I was at knowing what the boys in the Tea Room would go for. I understood those from the coal pits and I understood those from the universities. But I have no vision of the future."

I helped with the leadership program, but my main assignment was to set up my program on Public Services Redesign. I began running one public service area after another through the conceptual framework I'd developed during my sabbatical. Jody Hauer and Margo Stark helped with solid research and with the thinking. We focused not on state agencies, which account for quite a small proportion of the budget, but on the local agencies (partly financed by the state) which do most of the work: child day care; transit, housing, the fire service, public safety, waste collection and disposal. We did look at the postal service; literally 'the delivery system'. We mailed PSRP memos and notes from interviews to a growing list of persons locally and around the country.

Though not properly faculty, I got to offer a seminar on 'redesign' that helped me learn how to explain the concepts to others. 'Fire Control' turned out to be a wonderful case. Write "preventing loss from fire" on the blackboard; ask students then to think out the elements of that system. Obviously, put out the fire. OK: How? Shoot streams of water from the street. Fine: How many professional fire departments are there to do that in Minnesota? Only a handful? Oh. What are the others? Volunteers. OK. Will hoses work for tall buildings? No? What, then? Sprinklers. OK. How else prevent loss? Keep the valuables safe from fire. Sure. If fires do start, keep them from spreading. Right. That gets us into building materials. Keep fires from starting. Of course. What or who starts fires? What are the incentives in this system? Where does insurance fit in? Inspection? Pretty soon everyone sees that 'the fire brigade', the municipal fire service, is a small part of the fire-control system. (Jody did a memo on "The Declining Need for the Fire Department" that caused some considerable stir in Saint Paul City Hall.)

The growing interest in 'alternative service delivery'

Both the inflation of the '70s and the recession following in the early '80s pushed this discussion. The PSRP project got me involved with others discussing 'alternative service delivery': Dave Lyon, running the domestic side of RAND, Steve Waldhorn at SRI, Lester Salamon at the Urban Institute. Homer Wadsworth and John Gardner were setting up The Independent Sector. The Aspen Institute organized a conference at Wye Plantation, at which I met Jack Clarke, an executive at Exxon, who gave my project one of the grants infamous at the company's education foundation. He was responsible, I heard, for law, public affairs, health care and the Middle East. A couple of years later, when I stopped by to thank him, I said something about the conflict there. "It just gets a little worse all the time", he said.

The trip to Copenhagen in the summer of '80 was organized by the University's Center for Urban and Regional Affairs. We stayed at the training center for International Service Systems; ate herring and drank Carlsberg; spent a lovely warm evening at Tivoli listening to Perlman and Zukerman. We got to understand the squeeze being felt by "the small welfare states". I heard about and visited Falck—the Danish private fire-service company.

The following year, on a grant from the German Marshall Fund, the MANCs bought the house at Ditchley for a weekend discussion. The locals who came had been arguing all week in London about the same questions: Terry Heiser, the permanent secretary of the Department of the Environment, John Stevenson heading the Association of County Councils, Roy Shaw on the Labour side, from Camden and on the board of The Audit Commission. Simon Jenkins, then political editor of The Economist.

One of the Europeans I brought in was Jan Assentorp, in charge of planning for Falck. They had contracts with about half the municipalities in Denmark. "Have you ever lost a contract once you had it?" someone asked. "No", he said. Henk van Ruller came; former city manager of Amsterdam. To general surprise he told us Schipol airport is a private corporation. Then clarified: The shareholders are the Government of The Netherlands, the Province of North Holland and the City of Amsterdam. Sometimes private structures work better: "We Dutch are pragmatic."

In Minnesota, Governor Perpich in 1982 launched an effort to improve productivity in state government; got William Andres, then just retired as CEO of Dayton-Hudson, to chair it. Andres began by asking people: *Is productivity something you do . . . or something that happens if you do the fundamentals right?* "I was in retailing", he would say. "In retailing turnover is very important. Every so often we get a store manager who tries to *do* turnover. Quickly that store isn't profitable any longer. So we decided turnover is some-

Is productivity something you do . . . or something that happens?

thing that happens and that we would try to do the fundamentals right." That distinction was to prove important.

Fairly quickly pressures from public-employee labor turned the 'P' in the governor's program from 'productivity' into 'performance'. To labor 'productivity' meant the speed-up. I got a lesson about labor pressure later that year when I went with delegations of city managers to Germany and to Japan. Riding the bus in Japan Bob Kipp told me about his effort in Kansas City to staff the fire stations relative to the incidence of fires—most of which occur there in the hour after midnight—and how the firefighters had killed that effort. At the meeting in Bonn I began what became a lasting acquaintance with Gerhard Banner, heading KGSt, an internal consultancy for German local government.

In '83, on a visit to London, John Stevenson took me to a reception in The Banqueting House just across Downing Street from No. 10; the ceiling entirely covered with paintings by Reubens. Curious about The Audit Commission, I asked if its controller, John Banham, was here. "If he were you'd know it", Stevenson said. I did go by its office; got acquainted with its program for an annual performance audit of local government functions. Later got to know his successor, Howard Davies.

In the presidential campaign in 1984 Senator Gary Hart drew considerable national attention with his talk about 'new ideas'. One of his staff called at some point. I asked what kind of ideas they were looking for. "Well, like 221(d)3", he said. My God, they're looking for *program* ideas! In November, hoping to get at *strategic* ideas, our project brought people to Saint Paul for a conference on "An Equitable and Competitive Public Sector".

At some point a group of Fabians came here. Contracting violated their good socialist principles. I mentioned to one that I'd read about an old people's home run by the National Health Service where one summer day the staff had set out a cold beef salad and 27 people had died. There was to be an investigation. I asked what was the outcome. "A law was passed saying if something like that happens you can sue", he said. "What do you think the accountability would have been if the salad had been served by a contract operator?" I asked. "Point" he said, in the English way.

In 1990 Richard Murray, working on public sector productivity as economist for the Statskontoret, brought me over to talk to the summer retreat of managers in the Swedish national government, at Linkjoping.

David Osborne came through, doing research for what became **Reinventing Government** in 1992. The book gave a nice compliment to Minnesota. It sold an almost unheard-of quarter-million copies. David's subsequent experience in Washington with the Clinton administration was not entirely happy. His project was housed with the National Academy of Public Administration. "Public administrators *don't want* to reinvent government", David said to me a few years later.

'Voice' and 'exit'—the dynamics of change

Gradually interest spread and understanding developed. Something like this was, simply, necessary. And surely possible. Options ... alternatives ... choices ... "many producers" ... As the discussion went on it became ever-clearer that redesign, any successful effort to deal with the problems of cost and quality, and of change, implied a competitive public sector.

As he was leaving The Audit Commission In 1992, Howard Davies set out the fundamentals of his experience with performance evaluation in the little book he wrote for the Social Market Foundation: **Fighting Leviathan.** "*Successful public sector agencies need to adopt the same characteristics as successful private concerns. They need to be responsive to their customers and constantly in search of efficiency gains and quality improvements. These desirable characteristics cannot be imposed*", he wrote: "*They are created by forces that impose competitive pressure.*"

How to acknowledge this, yet make it persuasive, even appealing?

Nothing proved more useful than what Albert Hirschman had written in 1971 in **Exit, Voice and Loyalty.** Subtitled **Responses to Decline in Firms, Organizations and States**, his small classic illuminated the importance of choices.

The essential idea works powerfully for the strategy of options. In a neighborhood, a business, a church, in any organization, one response to decline is to stay and talk it out. Many do that. Some instead leave. Every system needs both voice and exit. The exit of quality members empowers the voice of those who remain: Their voice is essential to make the exit of the others effective. Where exit is suppressed, voice is ignored. But exit can also deprive organizations of their most effective voices. So, organizations, must continually be searching for that "elusive optimal mix" of exit and voice.

Where exit is suppressed, voice is ignored

On a swing east, taking our son to visit colleges, I went to see Hirschman at the Institute for Advanced Study. He had written the book, he said, to persuade economists, interested mainly in 'exit', of the usefulness of 'voice'. He had been surprised by the interest it created among political scientists, whose field is 'voice', in the potential of 'exit'.

The ideas were falling into place. Consequences matter, for organizations. Organizations that face no consequences can safely put their own interests first; will feel no compulsion to change. 'Exit' creates consequences; so needs to be present to create an incentive for change.

That required attention to politics, and highlighted the importance of a strong civic sector for system change. "To be workable," Lester Thurow wrote in 1980 in **The Zero-Sum Society**, "*a democracy assumes that public decisions are made in a framework where there is a substantial majority of concerned but disinterested citizens who will prevent policies from being shaped by those with direct economic self-interests.*" In **The Economic Prerequisite for Democracy** in 1980 Daniel Usher warned about the reverse; a situation in which more than half the people have their incomes politically determined.

The question was how to design incentives—reasons and opportunities—for organizations to change, and to develop 'settings' in which that work of system-design could be carried on. Monnet, in his **Memoirs**, wrote that "I had come to see it was often useless to make a frontal attack on problems, since they have not arisen by themselves but are the product of circumstances. Only by modifying the circumstances—lateral thinking—can one disperse the difficulties they create. So I had become accustomed to seeking out and trying to change whatever in its environment was causing the block."

Walter McClure put it simply: "Institutions and organizations tend to behave the way they're structured and rewarded to behave. If you don't like the way they're behaving, you probably ought to change the way they're structured and rewarded".

CHAPTER 15:

What Alternatives?
How Created?

Getting the new concepts into use required explaining, first, what are the alternative ways of doing things; then explaining how to get them into use.

The challenge was to show governors and legislators how to give the operating systems—medical-hospital...social and human services...public education...post-secondary education...transportation...city and county government—reasons and opportunities to be seeking "efficiency gains and quality improvements" on their own initiative, in their own interest and from their own resources.

That took us back to William Andres: What are the fundamentals that will cause the operating organizations to do improvement? That highlighted the difference between the private sector and the public. A private business takes the competitive world as a given. For a public entity it is necessary first to introduce the idea of options, the opportunity for exit, to create the incentives for change.

Let's start with the alternative arrangements; then move to the question of how to get them introduced.

What are the other ways of 'doing things'?

The default arrangement is service; hiring people to do things for others for pay. The first eight below are *alternatives to* that 'service' model; the final three are *variations on* the 'service' model. You might be surprised to see so many alternatives, but there are always more shoes in the back room than the salesman tells you there are. Also, the distinctions are arbitrary; one often contains some element of another.

1. **'Load-shedding'**—Sometimes things really don't need to be done at all, or can't be justified any longer. Minneapolis' public works department had a non-working foreman on every job no matter how small. Uniformed officers used to fill out insurance reports on fender-bender accidents. Sometimes the work really can be turned back to individuals and families. On Minnesota's Iron Range it probably wasn't essential for city crews to plow private gardens.

2. **Prevention**—If a problem doesn't appear in the first place there'll be no need to spend money to hire professionals or to buy expensive technology to fix it. Prevention has potential in many areas; avoiding the higher costs that come with expensive service or 'repair'. 'Workers compensation' is a classic example of prevention: The system redesign that made employers responsible for the cost of accidents induced businesses to make workplaces safer. Over the 20 years after the initial law in the state of Washington had introduced the idea nationally, the injury rate in the iron and steel industry fell by 90 percent. Firemen don't much like doing inspections, but preventing fires makes basic sense. An OECD report saw that changing behavior is often a key to 'prevention': No staff of street-sweepers can keep a city clean if people are determined to walk along shedding paper. The public's health, too, depends largely on the way people behave. So government works to persuade people not to litter, to stop smoking, to drive safely.

3. **Supported self-help**—It's not Downton Abbey any more. Few of us today can afford cooks, gardeners, maids, chauffeurs,

seamstresses and governesses. Domestic service has evolved into do-it-yourself arrangements. Someone sells us the equipment, materials, designs, and training; we put in the labor. For many things DIY now substitutes for expensive professional service. Betty Crocker's cookbook and somebody's mixers. You bought a car and learned how to drive. Toro helped you take care of your lawn. Singer made sewing machines, JoAnn sold fabrics and someone sold patterns. Rosetta Stone can help you learn Italian.

4. **Mutual help**—People have always done things to help each other, in families and in neighborhoods. Care for children. Drive old folks around. Read to students; advise, mentor. Keep an eye on property. Braid hair. Often voluntary associations, 'mediating structures', organize these efforts. Informal arrangements attract the opposition of professionals and commercial operators. They try to install 'certification' requirements to make it illegal for ordinary people to help each other or to do things together. Producer groups want to 'fence out' what they see as competition. Happily, a few persons fight credentialing; try to slow the spread of licensing requirements.

5. **Co-production**—Involve the clients, consumers, citizens themselves in the work of meeting their needs. Physicians can often get their patients helping with therapy, or train them to give themselves shots (as an alternative to coming in for the doctor to do it). There is huge potential for teachers to get their students actively involved in their own learning—or in getting students to help other students (peer teaching). Digital electronics, and the new 'sharing economy', are now changing and enlarging the concept of co-production and mutual help.

6. **Utilization**—Where service work contains periods of 'down time' it's possible to fill in the gaps with other work. Smaller cities have volunteer fire departments: People drop their regular work when the alarm rings and meet the truck at the fire. Big-city fire departments with full-time personnel have lots of 'down time'; so their employees have become

paramedics.. Falck might be the ultimate example. See www. Falck.com. Recently the cellphone 'apps' are connecting people who need a service with people who can provide a service; as with Uber and Lyft and AirBnB. Carpooling is utilization: the vehicle is going anyway; might as well fill it up.

7. **Substitution**—Sometimes a service that operates at lower cost can be substituted for one that operates at higher cost. So: hospice care rather than hospital care, nurse practitioners rather than MDs; plow snow rather than remove snow, melt snow rather than plow snow; hire civilians rather than sworn officers to read parking meters. There's also, of course, a 'substitution' strategy with respect to equipment; low-capital strategies rather than high-capital strategies. Install fluorescent rather than incandescent lighting, now LEDs rather than fluorescents.

8. **Regulation**—Often this is seen as simply a way to stop bad things from happening. But it can work also as a way to get private parties to do things the government decides should be done but chooses not to do itself. Government provides us with clean restaurants not by cleaning them itself but by requiring their owners to keep them clean at their own expense.

9. **Private provision**—Neighborhood (and non-geographic) groups can contract for services that in some contexts would be considered public. I asked Mayor Latimer once how the snow gets out of Saint Paul alleys. "Damned if I know", he said. In fact, the people who live along the block take up a collection and hire someone with a plow on the front of his 4x4 to come through after it snows. Those putting on athletic contests often contract for security; sometimes with a private firm—and sometimes with the local city police.

10. **Volunteering**—Many people will do service work for public and quasi-public organizations without charge. Both government units and nonprofits commonly make use of volunteers. Think: roadside litter pickup; hospital auxiliaries; museum docents; tutors in school. Sometimes those you get

are professionals, sometimes they are amateurs. Sometimes it doesn't make much difference.

II. **Consolidation** — Be careful about this: Organizing service at larger scale does not necessarily change the way things are done, and there is truth in the experience that "size breeds cost". But there sometimes are economies of scale, unnecessarily high costs that can be reduced if operations are combined. Minnesota's Joint Powers law opens this direction, now letting two governmental units to do together what *either* can do alone. Beware the assumption, though, that consolidation on the operating side necessarily requires also a consolidation on the policy side.

How can policy introduce these alternatives?

So, then: How would policy bodies introduce the 'competitive pressures' that—per Howard Davies—would cause the operating bodies continually to be seeking quality improvements and efficiency gains? There seemed to be several approaches, all involving the design of incentives, the reasons and opportunities provided for change.

I. **Introduce contract arrangements**—The operating agencies tend to think more clearly about controlling costs and being responsive when they cannot take their customers for granted. So break out of arrangements like the public bureau that permit the operator to take the buyer—citizens or elected officials—for granted. Be wary of anyone saying a solutions must be all-or-nothing; either this-way or that-way; no choices. Avoid sole-source contracting. Work for the mixed arrangements that are possible. A policy body can contract for only a part of its work, continuing to use its administration for the rest. A policy body can contract for all or part of the service with other governmental organizations. The opposite, of course, is also possible: Where a city 'buys' it can introduce the option to 'make': More than one city has owned an asphalt plant it did not operate, as a way of encouraging competitive bids from its commercial suppliers.

2. **Run the money down the consumer side**—Stop appropriating money to the bureau or to contractors to give expensive professional services for free. Instead, run the financing to the users and let them select the vendor. Hennepin County (which did not do child care itself) did essentially this in the 1980s when it stopped contracting with child-care centers and gave families money with which to buy care. Parents could then choose either center care or family care. Family care is usually less expensive, so offering that option meant more children could be served. It's what we do with food stamps. Higher education is priced to its users, with student aid need-based. These programs can be universal or selective; in the latter case, arranged to require those who can pay to do so, focusing limited resources on helping those who genuinely cannot.

3. **Broaden the range of vendors available**— To make the 'consumer-side' strategy most effective, diversify and expand the number of choices available to citizens eligible. Indigent people used to have to go to the local public hospital. Now they may choose the clinic and hospital they prefer. Children used to be required to attend the schools of the district—or even the school of the attendance area—in which they lived. Public policy in many states has now moved to 'open enrollment'; inter- and intra-district choice.

4. **Capitate producers**—Give the operating organization a lump sum and a clear charge to perform and let them keep what they don't need to spend. In Milwaukee Superintendent Howard Fuller—faced with a problem of teacher-absences—gave the schools a lump sum for substitutes. Teacher absences went down, reducing the need for substitutes. Capitation could be designed to let the employees keep as personal income part of the savings they generate.

5. **Decentralize**—Delegate decision-making to front-line units better able to know what users need. Set general objectives for

learning, say, and let schools decide how students will learn. This can be combined with capitation. When schools pay their own electricity bills and can use whatever they save for school activities, energy bills go down. When our Legislature let suburbs 'at the end of the bus line' keep the revenue from the Twin Cities transit tax those municipalities redesigned service to meet local needs. When given authority and trusted to make decisions, people usually will respond with better effort.

6. **Deregulate**—Over the years the notion of 'public convenience and necessity' has been used to limit the number of operators and to reduce the competition among them. The taxi industry has been notorious for this; the limitation on licensing vastly inflating the cost of a medallion, the permission to drive. In the Twin Cities area the Metropolitan Airports Commission effectively ended the old system when it required any cab to take a passenger to any destination. In the 1970s, when chairman of the CAB, Alfred Kahn deregulated the airlines. Today far more people fly and at lower real cost.

7. **Withdraw the 'exclusive'**—Where a local unit or level of government fails to get its operations moving, it is sometimes possible for the state to create some new entity that will: a new 'provider'. State governments did this in the 1990s: Frustrated by the school districts' failure to redesign, states created a new, second sector in public education with the chartering laws. (See Chapter 18.) Something similar happened when, in disposing of the plants built during World War II, the government created a corporate rival to Alcoa as a way of improving market behavior in the aluminum industry. And be sure to avoid organizing new public services as territorial exclusive franchises.

The politics of introducing new arrangements

In 1986 Harlan Cleveland suggested I try to get this analysis into the Public Administration Review. I wrote an article that ran in the summer issue as "The Two Different Concepts of Privatization".

The article challenged the conventional thinking that assumed government must itself do whatever is decided should be done. In it I asked readers to see the essential function of government as using public money or public authority to ensure that something happens. 'Producing' that outcome might be governmental or might not. Even were it not, the action would be public; the test of 'public' being the decision to provide.

I concluded by saying: *"For the moment, both the private leadership and the political leadership are mired in the old ways of thinking. . . . A new concept, combining equity in the provision of services with competition in their production has yet to be articulated politically."* We will come back to this in Chapter 22.

Clearly a big job remained, to explain the provider/producer distinction and to justify the use of alternatives. There was a need, also, to show those in policy roles how to introduce the different arrangements successfully.

Gradually these answers emerged.

- **Set up the thinking about productivity-improvement separate from whatever group is working to solve the budget crisis.** For those caught in a budget crisis reality is what can be done *now*. Tax and cut appear the only options available, so these people are bound to dismiss redesign. The longer-term system restructuring has to be assigned to units and persons *not* involved in the budget-balancing; in the executive branch and in the legislative branch.

- **Accept that the timing will often be out of phase.** By the time alternative arrangements are designed the fiscal crisis might have passed. Hey, the rain has stopped: Why do we need this umbrella? Insist: Rain will come again; the state needs to be ready.

- **Be clear at the start that this work will take time.**
  Have patience. Get some smart younger people for this
  'redesign' job and plan for them to work at it for four years
  minimum; perhaps as many as 10. Some should be inside
  state government: in the planning agency, possibly in the
  Department of Finance. Perhaps in a new unit. Some should be
  set up outside the government: There are just some issues that
  cannot be effectively raised inside; that have to be pressed from
  a non-political position outside.

- **Communicate general ideas as well as examples.** General
  ideas have no effect without examples to make them 'real'.
  But equally it is ineffective to work just with specifics; without
  the general ideas that create "a place in the head" where
  policymakers can make sense of the new proposals. Powerful
  images help. The no-smoking ordinances began to come
  in Minnesota when the Minneapolis Tribune's restaurant
  reviewer wrote: "If you can smoke in the air I breathe, I can spit
  in your soup."

- **Make clear this is not 'privatization'.** It's not privatization
  when the county contracts for the management of its
  hospital. Or when it closes its hospital and buys care from the
  community hospitals. *It is privatization when the county says it
  will no longer pay for the care of those needing financial support.*
  The 'public' function lies in the decision to provide; in using
  public resources and/or public authority to ensure that a thing
  will be done. As, with the GI Bill. *The test of 'public' does not lie in
  the governmental or non-governmental character of the organization
  used to produce, to deliver, the service.*

- **Learn how to 'buy right'.** When some effort to buy service
  goes bad the response is usually to blame the contractor. But
  often it's the fault of the buyer, who does not know how to write
  good specs or how to inspect the work. At the University of
  Minnesota neither the school or management nor the school
  of public affairs taught a course in contracting. They taught
  students how to run things. I asked: "Do managers ever buy

things?" Answer: They do. "But we don't teach them how to do that well?" No, we don't. The examples of buying-smart are impressive. At the Minneapolis housing authority Don Jacobson specified wooden frame around the metal windows. Under union rules that meant the windows would be installed by carpenters." A carpenter knows what a quarter-inch is", Don said. "He'll plane the window to fit. A metalworker will take a hammer and hit it." For years the Minneapolis towing contract was a scandal: cars broken into, charges exorbitant. Annually the contract had been renewed with one company for the north half of the city, with another for the south. A towing company had to own an impoundment lot. No competitor was going to acquire a lot just to qualify to bid. The city redesigned the specs. It got its own impoundment lot; contracted only for the towing. It got lots of new bidders; let four contracts. No company could win more than one. Problem solved.

- **Acknowledge candidly that the new will be imperfect.** Nobody gets everything right on the first try. Everyone will understand this. Ask them to think about the first auto, the first airplane, the first computer, the first cellphone. The first anything. Over time most improve.

- **Think in 'system' terms.** Paul Hill was with RAND when we first met. I asked: How do you define 'a system'? "A collection of interacting parts", he said. This suggests a concept of system change: Alter one part and the others will adjust in response. But, which 'part'? Where to begin? "Start with the initiative that creates the most pressure for other constructive changes": Murnane and Levy in **Teaching the New Basic Skills** cite that advice from Hirschman. This was Monnet's strategy for European integration. (See page 161.) "One cannot act in general terms", he wrote, "but anything becomes possible when one can concentrate on *one precise point which leads on to everything else*." For him that was "the limited delegation of sovereignty that pooled the coal and steel industries of Germany and France", as his biographer wrote. Done successfully that created a 'dynamic disequilibrium' that led on to further integration.

- **Understand that systems change gradually.** It is impossible to change a system all at once. Not everyone agrees, or is ready now for the different. Proposals to change comprehensively will be resisted by many of those directly affected. The change that is possible will be incremental. (See page 217 on Everett Rogers and 'diffusion'.) That does not mean it cannot be radical: radical change *is* gradual. Horses gave way gradually to tractors; computers gradually replaced typewriters. Also, the more voluntary it is, the more radical it can be. And this radical change is sometimes rapid: Think cellphones. The right image for change is of a 'split screen'; the new model spreading at the same time as the traditional is improving, people moving from the old to the new as they decide themselves they are ready. In Section Six we will see this idea applied to education.

- **Work with causes, not with symptoms.** Don't let the current controversies pull you into attacking directly the bad-things-being-done. Avoid attacking the people: It is unfair and ineffective to blame people for responding rationally to the incentives set for them. Find what is causing the bad things to be done and the good things not to be done, *and fix that*. Understand how the system works; find the incentives; think how to change those.

- **Be careful not to get things wrong.** It surely is possible to do less for more. If you give organizations the wrong incentives— give them reasons and opportunities to run up costs to their own benefit—they surely will. And it will take years to recover. So beware of those saying how much better they could serve you if they only did not have to compete for your custom. Do not be romanced about 'economies of scale'. Be alert for proposals that create cost-pass-through arrangements. Be skeptical when assured that some expensive technology is the answer.

- **Be skeptical about 'research'.** It's common to hear that policy should be based on 'what research shows works'. That sounds sensible. But beware. Research looks for 'measures of central tendency', talks about 'overall' and 'on balance' and 'most' and 'by and large'. That misses the single cases of new-and-different that disprove its generalizations. Consider: In 1903 research was conclusive: heavier-than-air craft cannot fly. All the efforts had failed; all the contraptions had crashed. So what difference did that evidence make once Wilbur and Orville had got it right, had found the 'how'? Clearly a huge challenge for research is to pick up the innovations that challenge the existing data.

- **Beware 'Baumol'.** A prominent economist argued that productivity is impossible in the service sector. Consider a Mozart string quartet: Would you drop the second violin? Have the players play twice as fast? As always, look for the hidden premises. The argument assumes that to hear the music I must hear the music live; drive on a snowy night, pay to park, buy the tickets, sit while the person next to me rattles his program. If you think this is the only way to hear the quartet then of course costs will rise. But technology has provided other ways to hear the quartet. I can buy a CD and listen at home as often as I like. And it is possible now for a small fee to watch performances on the internet, with close-ups of performers' solos; perhaps that very Mozart string quartet. The Berlin Philharmonic, I'm told, does this today. This might be considered efficiency gain and quality improvement; might represent productivity.

- **Persist.** Never give up. Don't be discouraged by those—always around—who say, "It can't be done". Usually that means, "It can't pass this session". Of course it can't. Success requires building a base of understanding. That takes time. After the start there will be a slow and steady process of development. Progress will be uneven. But—Monnet again—"When one is sure of the outcome one can afford to be patient".

The central importance of getting the design right

Every time I drive up the ramp from downtown Saint Paul onto westbound I-94 I think it teaches us a lesson.

The ramp has two lanes merging as it enters a tunnel. While it was being built I stood one day with a highway engineer looking down at it from a window in the Kelly Inn; agreeing the curve coming out of the tunnel was designed too tightly. Sure enough: After the ramp opened, cars began crashing into its walls and guard-rails. In response the DOT put up (by my count) 19 yellow signs, including a three-foot-long arrow, telling drivers to slow down, move right, be careful. Still, drivers kept crashing; crews had to keep repairing the guard-rail. (Recently the DOT removed part of the guard-rail: Drivers who miss the turn presumably would now go off the road and down the hill into the trees. But no: As I write, the guard-rail is again wrecked.)

The lesson? That *regulation does not overcome the effects of bad design*. It is a hard lesson to get across: Nothing seems to shake the touching faith some have, that 'better regulation' is the right response when problems appear.

But good design does matter—and in other fields of activity as well. Al Godward remembered that, when a young draftsman laying out the roads in Minneapolis' Glenwood Park, Theodore Wirth looked over his

Regulation does not overcome the effects of bad design

shoulder one day saying, "Make the grades steep and the curves tight. We don't want any trucks on those parkways."

The lesson can be extended to systems. Their design determines how effectively, efficiently and responsively the organizations in them will behave. Rather than exhorting and ordering the organizations to behave well, arrange the system incentives so they will find it in their interest and will decide themselves to behave well. When you heard John Brandl say, "Structure is prior to management", this is what he had in mind.

It is essential to think about design, and to get the design right. Watch out for people who want to short-cut the process. Look again at the cycle diagram on page 154. Always there is someone wanting to cut directly from 'issue identification' to 'policy action', picking up the current, conventional 'solution'—which is often some expensive professional service or some big machine. Too many policy discussions are filled with zombie ideas; the walking dead.

All of this of course forces the question: Who is going to do the work, design the options and the incentives?

Which takes us to that matter of the 'settings'.

CHAPTER 16:

'Settings'– for thinking out the 'how'

Earlier I said the thinking about redesign goes on in what I suggested we call 'settings'. I mean this not in a geographic or an organizational sense, but to identify the combination of opportunity, time, financing and independence provided for persons to explore the 'why' of problems and to develop the 'how' of solutions. To consider how systems are organized, how they work, how they sometimes fail, how they might be redesigned and reconstructed. Clearly this work can take many organizational forms, and can be done in many locations.

Let's go back to that initial graphic. In it the work of the 'settings' appears 'at about eight o'clock' on left side of the 'policy cycle'; analyzing the cause of the problem and developing the proposal for redesign.

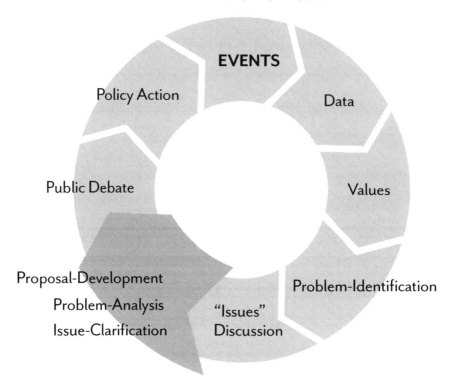

Perhaps it will help, will convey an understanding of their importance, to discuss a few of these settings briefly.

The Citizens League as a 'setting'

The Citizens League as it existed and operated into the 1980s was doing essentially this kind of work; in those years possessed the key characteristics I'm talking about.

- It had sustaining financing, largely from several thousand individual members and several hundred business firms acting as citizens. Study projects were not financed separately. That permitted the organization to decide itself what questions it would take under study. Its practice was to inquire broadly which problems various groups thought were important to study. Contributors were good about not pressing the League to enter, or avoid, particular areas.

- It had an unusual set of people involved in an unusual process. This was not an academic research operation, though some university people did sign up to be members of a study committee (one of them later a Nobel laureate in economics). The work attracted mainly those interested in working with abstractions. The League had the—uncompensated—services of concerned and experienced citizens from different walks of life. And was able to call on, and to receive (again, uncompensated) advice and background from those in operating roles and policy roles in public life. Paul Gilje described the process best, in "**The Citizens League Itself**", still available on the League's website.

- The organization had—had earned, over time—the respect that provided the independence necessary; earned this from a community sense that the organization, while by no means a cross-section of the population, stood outside the normal interest groups and special interests. This helped its analysis to be attended-to and its advice quite often to be adopted. Getting its ideas around was important, so it was critical of course for the newspapers to be covering the serious policy discussion. Both were elements of the civic system.

- It attracted a remarkably dedicated and hard-working staff; initially lawyers and then for a while journalists; later—but not necessarily—graduates of a school of public affairs. Curious. Able to work comfortably with academics, with elected officials, with administrators, with researchers, with volunteers. You worked when volunteers were available: There were a lot of breakfast and evening meetings; a lot of 15-hour days.

- At the start, in the way of traditional municipal-reform organizations, the League tried to endorse 'good people' for public office. It found this difficult and not productive; quickly dropped it and the budget-analysis traditional in these organizations in favor of focusing on governmental structure, on the incentives created by the system-arrangements.

- It relied for its effectiveness on persuasion; having no money to donate and no votes to deliver; relying mainly on the relevance and timeliness and good sense of its proposals.

- It was proactive about getting its information around. Its Tuesday morning breakfasts and Q&A luncheon meetings were open to the public; were well attended, and were reported by the League itself in the CL News. As early as 1966 it developed the practice of mailing the full discussion minutes of its committee meetings not only to committee members but also to others interested in following the discussion about the topic under study. At a study-committee meeting we could often see in the audience key persons from other organizations or the public agencies interested and involved.

- The League thought the policy process should compromise decisions and not compromise proposals. It thought the discussions of public affairs were best made diverse as different groups with different perspectives and different objectives were in their own way and in their own frameworks analyzing problems and generating proposals, then advancing their arguments in open public and legislative debate. Its study committees were not composed of 'the stakeholders', nor did it see its projects as an effort to reconcile the interested positions of the various stakeholders. The League made its own judgment about the problem, about what was needed and what was possible; about how far others could be persuaded. It did not circulate its reports before release to other organizations interested or potentially affected. This left study committees free to challenge conventional thinking; playing the civic role that, as Verne had advised, was essential for meaningful change.

Other 'settings', in Minnesota and elsewhere

Over time, you do notice other such 'settings'; present and past, here and elsewhere. Here are four that I think were of special significance.

InterStudy: Redesigning the 'health care' system

Paul Ellwood, a neurologist in rehabilitation medicine, had come to Minnesota to head the Kenny Institute. He developed an interest in an integrated system of care; moved out of Kenny to form first the American Rehabilitation Foundation and then InterStudy to figure out how to create such a system.

Impressed by Kaiser-Permanente in California, he and Walter McClure thought out 'managed care'; originated what became the 'health maintenance organization'. Beginning with General Mills and the St. Louis Park Clinic the idea grew rapidly and soon Minnesota had the highest proportion of any state in prepaid plans. An ad in the Wall Street Journal brought Rich Burke to InterStudy. Quickly picking up the idea, he left to form Charter Medical, which evolved into what is today UnitedHealth Group.

One Saturday morning in 1983 Paul came to the Humphrey Institute for an interview about leadership, about policy and about InterStudy's role as a change-agent. This generated a set of notes—a copy of which I later gave his son when David was dean of the Kennedy School. Listen to the bells it rings.

- *I never thought of myself as a leader; never held office or had money to give away. Everything has depended on getting others to make change . . . My first thought was to move toward government . . . but the more I read the more I became concerned that planning and regulatory approaches would be captured by those you set out to regulate . . . I became aware of Kaiser-Permanente in California; the way it combined everything into a single payment for care . . . InterStudy moved to a strategy of using incentives to cause organizations to change on their own . . .*

- *It is essential for these policy-study organizations to be turned outward; kept small, with low overhead. Size breeds cost... If you grow large you will depend on outside support... Our best work was done after we became independent. It is essential to be independent. The best people are compulsive, hard-working, bright, committed; with broad interests, not specialized. Intuitive. They have good communications skills; write well and talk persuasively. These are better than quantitative skills... I am always pushing out ideas I half-understand. A key job is to put the meat on the bones of an idea. Walter McClure did this at InterStudy.*

- *Professional organizations are political organizations and not change-agents... You don't make change in a mass way. I learned that what you get are a few converts, who will make a difference... We learned that if a change has political implications or will take more than two years to accomplish, you'd better make it a-political... Business is a disappointment: A CEO explained to me: "You don't take on anything you might lose, especially if you have to do it in public"... It has been important not to alienate (the doctors). They are not 'bad people'. A direct attack on the professionals would not work... In service organizations it's the ordinary working stiff who delivers the product: If we undermine their professionalism we undermine the whole operation...*

- *I question how much of this can be learned. You have to be curious about why things work the way they do; and have this notion that you can maybe change it; have the right to change it... Models have been important to me; Theodore Vail at the telephone company, pushing change at the monopoly by creating Bell Labs to make the existing system obsolete... You find you can help these characteristics along in other people... You can't know at the start what is going to work, or how; you have a process of trial and error... Access to good information is the basis of whatever credibility you have... Probably the leader has to be a discontented professional... You have to see the problem a certain way and have a clear idea how you want to act. This might change as you learn, but you have to have a point of view... You obviously do become a promoter. But of the core idea; not of the specifics. You have to stay flexible; remain detached ...*

- *One major function is to facilitate the exchange of information locally and nationally among people working on the same problem or advocating a similar solution ... Patience is a great virtue. (At this point Ellwood had been working on this problem about 20 years.) ... You can also be helpful to the entrepreneurs trying something new. They are often isolated; frequently are low-status people in their field who need some recognition, support. In their case it can be an asset not to be 'professionally qualified' and therefore not to know that what they are trying to do 'can't be done'.*

Afterward, Paul said: "Nobody has ever had this conversation with me before".

General Mills: Assisted living

Occasionally important redesign appears in the non-governmental sector. One of the most interesting and significant was the redesign of ... the creation of alternatives within ... the housing system, to introduce what has come to be called 'assisted living'. This developed largely as Verne Johnson's initiative at General Mills, where he had gone in 1967 to head its corporate planning.

Verne did not want his public background to draw him into the company's government relations. Instead, he became involved in the thinking about General Mills' social role as an extension of his role in corporate planning. He and the vice chairman, Jim Summer, worked out a new concept of philanthropy. Unenthusiastic about writing checks to nonprofits, they evolved the concept of a business firm using its own management skills to do something socially useful; treating as its contribution the margin of normal profit foregone.

Initially they partnered with the Stevens Court housing project, an upgrading of apartments south of Minneapolis' downtown. The developer's use of non-union labor aroused the building trades, and faced with the prospect of opposition from the AFL-CIO General Mills withdrew.

What then? Verne had chaired the PSO project. He personally wanted to go into education; was able to spend a year traveling, interviewing and looking for the right opportunity. He was attracted by Jim Boyle and the computer-based program of remedial education Jim called Ombudsman. But the company executives, several of whom were then trying to find acceptable arrangements for their parents' late years, preferred to move to the problem of housing the frail elderly. Out of this developed the Altcare project; initially a partnership with Wilder Foundation then headed by Len Wilkening and then still focused on the elderly.

The problem was obvious. There was little if anything between the private home and the nursing home; between independent living and institutionalization. More and more of the elderly could not remain at home but could not afford, did not need or did not want full-time care. Altcare created the concept of an intermediate facility; essentially residential but with care on the premises, available for purchase in increments of time. Its story can be found in a case study available from the Center for Policy Design; based partly on the book Verne commissioned about Altcare and partly on an interview with the head of ALFA, the Assisted Living Federation of America, about the subsequent spread and evolution of assisted living all over America.

This is only to note the Altcare project as a 'setting'; providing the time, support and encouragement for a team of individuals to think out a new solution. Remarkably, financed by a business corporation.

The Carnegie Corporation: Re-setting the discussion about race

At the urging of Newton Baker, one of its trustees, the Carnegie Corporation in the mid-1930s organized a project to examine race relations in America; "the Negro problem", as was then said. The project had all the key elements: people, time, financing and freedom to challenge conventional thinking.

In his preface to **An American Dilemma** the foundation's president, Frederick Keppel, described the decision in 1937 to bring in a non-American, the Swedish economist Gunnar Myrdal, to head the project.

Keppel made available a staff that included many of the major figures in American sociology and political science. He rejected Myrdal's appeal for a commission to join him in the recommendations. Keppel insisted: The conclusions and recommendations will be yours alone.

The book appeared in 1944; the central idea distilled down to the few powerful opening pages and indeed into the title itself, expressing Myrdal's conviction that the problem was in fact in the mind and the heart of the white American; the 'dilemma' the disparity between "the American creed" of equality and the reality of the nation's treatment of its black citizens. This redefinition of the problem underlay the civil rights movement 10 years later and the civil rights legislation 10 years after that, and still shapes much of the discussion about race and public action in America 70 years after the book's publication.

Jean Monnet: The design of new European institutions

The son of a minor producer in Cognac, Monnet was sent off at age 16 to sell the family brandy in England and North America. Returning 10 years later, in 1914, he sought—and astonishingly got—an opportunity to explain to the prime minister of France that, to defeat Germany, Britain and France needed to merge their efforts. With his contacts and his understanding of the British, exceptional for a Frenchman at that time, he was given a key role in coordinating wartime Allied shipping and supply. The experience taught him the importance of cooperation among nations and started him into a major role in the design and creation of the new institutions of western Europe after World War II.

His death in 1981 got me reading the **Memoirs**. It is an astonishing explanation of how things happen in the public world; full of insights about changing the way people and politicians think. I bought some of the last copies in print and gave them to friends—one to Verne. "Turned me on for about a year", he said. Midge and I visited most of the places Monnet had lived: Cognac, Foxhall Road in Washington DC, Houjarry, outside Paris. We went into the planning commissariat in the Rue Martignac one August day: I asked to see the dining room. An agreeable young woman took us up to the little space in the attic. "This is still a very important room", she said.

The **Memoirs** is interesting personal life. It is one of the important histories of postwar Europe, Monnet describing his role in creating the Common Market and then the European Community. At a third level it is about how to integrate political communities; has parallels with Minnesota's metropolitan integration. At the deepest level it is about how things get done in public life, filled with the understanding that "problems have not arisen by themselves, but are the product of circumstances"; that success in solving problems requires changing the circumstances; 'lateral thinking'.

His 'setting' was supported for a time by the family's cognac business, in the postwar years by his role with De Gaulle as planning director for France (where his threats to resign helped maintain his independence), later by others financing the work on European integration.

Monnet was exceptional in combining civic and governmental roles: an individual citizen (with no more than a secondary-school education!) operating with great effect at the highest policy levels. "By all rights no one like this should ever have had any influence in France", I once heard a professor of European studies say.

The wide variety of local 'settings'

The more I reflect on it, the more conscious I am of the variety of 'settings' here, helping give Minnesota its superior capacity to adapt the institutions and arrangements of its public life.

Some, like the Citizens League, were general-purpose; some single-purpose. Some were permanent; some temporary, dissolved when their work was done. Some were associated with a particular individual; went away when that person moved, retired or died.

Once you see the concept, others appear. For example:

- Joe Robbie used the Legislative Commission on Municipal Laws to redesign the process for annexation and incorporation, generating the proposal for the Minnesota Municipal Commission.

- Jack Davies was an individual state senator when he developed the legislation moving auto insurance from a fault-based to no-fault system.

- Al Quie, when governor, worked with leaders in the Bar Association to create something more like a merit process for the selection of judges to replace the historic reliance on personal contacts and 'politics'. Rudy Perpich then used the new selection process, which included some non-lawyers, to bring in more women and people of color.

- Sometimes it is a membership association, like the League of Municipalities in which Orville Peterson worked out the redesign of the village code. Or the League of Women Voters, especially in Saint Paul when Ruby Hunt was active.

- Tony Simmons today at High School for the Recording Arts, working with the state and nationally to broaden the concept of achievement in evaluating schools serving over-age and under-credited young people.

- Art Rolnick, with his work on early-childhood education; a system designed around the idea of parent/client choice and including both a quality rating ("Parent Aware") and an evaluation carried out by SRI. Some of this began while he was still at the Federal Reserve Bank of Minneapolis.

- Sometimes it is an academic institution. The University of North Dakota was Wilson Laird's base when he persuaded that state's legislature to lay in, ahead, the management framework for the coming oil industry.

- Sometimes it is a professional group, like the lawyers who years ago developed the rules that drove the nepotism out of the Hennepin County bar; or more recently the committee adapting the law on 'common interest communities' in response to the spread of condominium ownership.

- Sometimes it is a single individual, or small group of individuals: Elmer Andersen, for example, instigating a revision in the method for selecting regents for the University of Minnesota. Or the three women who led the effort that resulted in Minnesota ending its state-hospital system for the mentally ill.

• • •

In the 1970s one big public system long exempted from the need to adapt came up for rethinking: public education. I need now to explain that system problem and the redesign that followed, and the 'setting' in which that work took place.

The cities had changed; racial integration was now at issue in the North as well as in the South; young people had changed; teachers were organizing to bargain collectively; falling test scores were causing the public to worry whether students were learning—all as the sense was developing that brainpower was becoming the key economic resource.

The report of the national commission in 1983—**A Nation At Risk**—was the principal 'event' that started 'education' moving around the cycle. The organization of administrators responded with a PR campaign: "Ah, those marvelous Minnesota schools"—meaning, I thought: Not a problem in Minnesota. "Invest in our children", the teachers union banners said, not for the first or last time.

But in fairly short order Minnesota began to see and think about the problem of school and system design. Those of us involved in the general discussion about redesign began to apply its concepts to elementary-secondary education. As we did, we felt the ideas and understandings going back to the PSO project could help with the 'why' for analysis and the 'how' for proposals.

Fairly quickly substantial changes began to be made. Education|Evolving became a 'setting' for that thinking, and education and its redesign became the focus of my own work for the succeeding 30 years.

SYSTEM CHANGE
IN PUBLIC EDUCATION

The redesign discussion in the '70s had missed public education. The K-12 system had been 'a castle on a hill', its issues reserved to its inhabitants who came out only for food and fuel—to get taxes raised and borrowings approved. Education had its own law, its own committees in the Legislature, its own governance, its own facilities, sometimes even its own election day. The 'school district' was a public utility headed by a professional who might hold office for 20 years. The major questions about the system's structure and operation were internal, not open for general public discussion.

Gradually in the '80s, stimulated by **A Nation At Risk**, the country began to see knowledge as the key resource, and old attitudes changed. A sense developed of the need to improve learning. This meant school would need to change. Perhaps also the system. That created the need to think about the 'how' of change, and this provided an opportunity to apply the emerging concepts of system redesign.

It was not an easy discussion. Educators displayed all the usual collective resistance to outside ideas. But as the criticism of the existing institution grew, thinking began about what a different K-12 system might look like, and how change could be made. New ideas appeared in Minnesota; some were copied around the country.

Chapter 17 describes the traditional system, brought by Horace Mann to America from Prussia in the mid-19th century, at the point where inter-district enrollment appeared in Minnesota. Chapter 18 explains the chartering idea; how it appeared and spread around the country, and how the opportunity to create new public schools made system change possible. Education|Evolving appears in Chapter 19 as the 'setting' that worked on system redesign. Chapter 20 describes its effort—begun in 2015 and still continuing) to enlarge teachers' professional responsibility by organizing public schools essentially as partnerships of teachers. Chapter 21 covers the national meetings centered on innovation, as more and more people began to ask, "Why always the same? Why not different?" In Chapter 22 the answer, and the strategy, come clear.

CHAPTER 17:

'School' Arrives on the Policy Agenda

In most states the school system stood outside general local government. East of the Alleghenies it appeared initially in the English pattern; an extension of town government north of the Mason-Dixon line and of county government to the south. But in most of the country public education came to be organized on the independent special district model.

The key elements and concepts of public education—age-grading, as an example—were fixed in the mid-19th century. Horace Mann had visited Prussia in 1843, had admired the bureaucratic system in that rising north German state and had brought the model back to Massachusetts. Spreading across the new western states, it became the dominant system; became 'real school' to generations of Americans. It is still the way 'school' is commonly illustrated: buildings with long hallways, oak doors opening into classrooms, desks in rows, a blackboard, an instructor. At one point Microsoft ran an ad—strangely ambiguous—promoting 'computers' but showing a conventional classroom in which neither computer nor teacher can be seen.

The administrative reforms of the early 20th century took education "out of politics"; bringing in a professional educator to 'superintend' the organization. In **Learning from L.A.** Charles Taylor Kerchner describes this autonomous institution created by the progressive era reform.

The proportion of young people getting a high school diploma roughly parallels the decades. After about 1916, as the child welfare movement took young people out of work, high school expanded dramatically. With the 'baby boom' after 1946 enrollments grew further. Small rural schools were gradually consolidated; usually as school districts were reorganized.

All this gave education a special status. General local government, certainly in Minneapolis, resented the schools' preferred access to public revenues. But into the 1960s the schools were strongly backed by business and civic groups and (cartoonists excepted) treated kindly by the media. On his wall our Tribune reporter had a row of 'School Bell' awards from the Minnesota School Boards Association. "The school board is the foundation of American democracy", their national director, Tom Shannon, preached into the 1980s. K-12 public education settled its own issues internally. There were as yet few serious questions being raised.

The discussion begins to be critical

'School' began to attract concern in the '60s. Books like **Why Johnny Can't Read** and **Up the Down Staircase** became popular. People began to wonder why 'teachers of the year' were so often let go, why SAT scores were falling. Strikes, and the battle over community control in New York City, made national news as teacher bargaining appeared and as neighborhoods pushed for greater control. Political change was beginning to erode the institutional arrangement Chuck Kerchner described.

As the pressure for change appeared, the system leadership was initially defensive. The head of our state superintendents' association (MASA) one day was insisting: "Education *does* change." When I pressed for an example he finally said: "Pregnancy leaves for teachers". When I suggested any change looks big when you're close to it, he exclaimed: "Well thank God education *doesn't* change!" When the Citizens League began to talk about accountability, site-based management and differentiated staffing it found superintendents tended to take questions as criticism and criticism as hostility: "You are not a friend of public education."

None of this critique found its way into Minnesota's re-equalization and re-financing of K-12 in 1971. But change was appearing.

About 1975 the Legislature enacted a tuition tax deduction. It was challenged in *Mueller v. Allen* but upheld by the U.S. Supreme Court— perhaps because it covered tuition paid to a public district as well as to a private school.

The idea of choice was appearing. Milton Friedman, and Coons and Sugarman in **The Case for Family Choice**, offered voucher proposals; public financing of education in non-public schools. The federal poverty program tried a voucher experiment at Alum Rock in California.

In Minneapolis, Dave Nasby persuaded his Saturday morning tennis partner, Superintendent John Davis, to contract for the education of students attending some of the nonprofit street-front 'alternative schools'.

It was a learning experience for me, watching change push at an institution so able to resist. I began to get drawn into discussion about the 'how' of change. I went on Governor Quie's task force in 1981. I was on the board at Spring Hill Center when we brought Jim Kelly here to be its president. Jim brought with him his experience with the education work of the Ford Foundation and the national network he had run as factotum of The Cleveland Conference.

Jack Coons was here early in '82. Curious to see if they could cope with his argument (*"Who knows most, cares most, about the child? Who will argue 'the state does'?"*) I arranged for him to talk with some superintendents and public-education advocates. They could not handle Jack's argument—or his defense of choice on equity grounds. (*"Some people have choice; others don't. The difference is money. We should standardize on one principle or the other: Either everyone should have choice, or no one should have it. As a liberal democrat I favor everyone having it."*)

Joe Nathan was stimulating talk about choice, with his book. He and I had a long evening with the four superintendents in north Ramsey County. "Why would anyone want to do that?" one asked. "Ninety-five per cent of our curriculum is the same."

The Education Commission of the States met in Minneapolis that summer. Bob Andringa invited me to the informal session the day after, with governors Robb and Graham and others, and John Gardner. They talked about the need to protect Albert Shanker; a statesman, they felt, working for change.

Willard Baker asked me to speak to the school boards association's August meeting. I mentioned the site-based budgeting in Florida; schools motivated to conserve energy because they could keep the savings for school activities. Joan Parent, a past president, turned to me afterward: "I'd never have handled it like that", she said. "I'd have sent them a directive to turn off the lights and turn off the air conditioning, and if they didn't do it I'd fire them!" Then turned and walked away.

Asked to moderate the governor's conference that fall, I solicited ideas for questions. Gerry Nelson, the AP capitol reporter, wondered: "Why does education have boundaries?" Many public services don't. At the break two farmers came up; not angry but wanting me to understand their reaction to the perspective Don Hill of the Minnesota Education Association (MEA) was presenting about compensation for teachers. We aren't guaranteed more every year, they said. Some years we lose money. Sometimes we lose the farm.

In the Humphrey Institute leadership seminar I came to know Dan Loritz, then in the Department of Education in a role that involved him with people wanting to cross district boundaries.

John Cairns had come in to head the new Minnesota Business Partnership (MBP). He and I formed Public School Incentives (PSI) to work in three areas: choice (Joe Nathan); site management, then a principals' cause (Lu Molberg) and teacher professionalism (Ruth Anne Olson), trusting teachers to know how the job should be done. All three ideas were to prove important. (We are all indebted to Lu for her advice about making decisions: "If you have to eat a frog it's best not to chew it.")

The idea of teachers as professionals was the least familiar of the three. But it was intriguing. In March '82 I brought people from law and medicine to an evening discussion, to which Gene Mammenga, lobbyist for the MEA, brought teachers. The teachers were fascinated by the 'partnership' arrangement; by the different working—and financial— relationship between professionals and administrators. I had to break up the meeting a little after 10 p.m. Nobody had moved. It was a school night. I sent the notes of the discussion around the country; getting responses variously enthusiastic, puzzled, intrigued, outraged.

In March '83 I drove Ron Hubbs to Rochester for a meeting with superintendents about site-management. During his time as CEO Hubbs had moved the St. Paul Companies to that model. He explained how and why decentralized operations work better. His audience was doubtful.

A Nation At Risk in 1983 brought education fully into the general policy discussion. At Shanker's urging the Carnegie Corporation created a Forum to do a response; Marc Tucker staffing the project that produced **A Nation Prepared**. It included a reference to the idea of teacher professional partnerships.

The National Education Association (NEA) brought its big national convention to Minneapolis twice in the '80s. Ted Sizer came, and we borrowed him to meet with locals. ("We can't *give* students an education", he said. "That they have to get for themselves.") Jim Kelly at Spring Hill enriched the local discussion; bringing in Mike Kirst, Allan Odden, Tucker, others.

More and more I saw these questions in the context of the earlier work on public services redesign: choices for citizens and for public officials, creating dynamics for change. At our 1984 meeting Luther Seabrook, former superintendent in Community District 5 in New York City talked about choice in central Harlem. Two schools were gaining enrollment; one was losing. That pattern, he said, the result of decisions by welfare mothers, "coincides precisely with my professional opinion about the relative merits of the three schools involved." In Wisconsin the school boards association was seeking the authority to contract. That began a long relationship with Senn Brown.

Public school choice: open enrollment and PSEO

For about seven years following the **A Nation At Risk** report there was much milling-around, much talk about 'restructuring', but no clear idea what that might mean beyond simple things like longer day and year or reducing class size in the early grades. But in Minnesota, coming to the '85 session, things crystallized.

Rudy Perpich had been elected governor in his own right in '82. In the '83 session he got the authority to appoint the commissioner of education. He brought in Ruth Randall. She talked up a storm about change. "High-tech, high-touch" and all that.

The Business Partnership had a task force working on education; chaired by Lewis Lehr, CEO of 3M Company. The study was contracted to Berman/Weiler. Paul Berman was sensing more potential for inter-district choice in Minnesota than in other states. In the summer of '84 Cairns called a small meeting to test the waters.

Berman drew Richard Green, the Minneapolis superintendent, into a debate with John Brandl, a DFL legislator favoring choice. Sensing the 'whether or not' argument was unproductive, I cut in; said to Green: Assume choice were introduced. What would Minneapolis do? Green said, "We'd compete like hell and we'd be damn tough". It was in this meeting that we first heard Arly Gunderman, recently president of the National Association of Elementary School Principals, make his stunning remark: "Candidly, my job as a principal is to motivate as much as I can, for as long as I can, people who are in essentially dead-end jobs".

In November the Partnership released its report. It did recommend inter-district choice. Lehr made appearances around the state presenting the report, trailed by the MEA president denouncing it.

In December, sitting with him in the back row at a Citizens League meeting, Perpich's policy advisor, Tom Triplett, said: "We're looking for an education program and we're not getting one"—meaning, from the department of education. We knew this from our summer discussions with the commissioner. So when PSI met it agreed the contact with Perpich should be through the finance department. We went to Gus Donhowe, its commissioner. A few days later came back the answer: OK, he'll do it. Curt Johnson worked with Loritz, soon to be Perpich's deputy chief of staff, on what was in effect a message to the Legislature, delivered in downtown Minneapolis.

Loritz drafted the bill Perpich really wanted. In the Senate Tom Nelson was the author. Connie Levi, the Republican House majority leader, signed on, conditional on Rudy including the post-secondary option she wanted. The media were dismissive: Why cover something all the groups oppose? But the bill came out of the education committee in both houses. When opponents removed inter-district enrollment in the tax committee the governor was irate; said that when he ran in '86 he would neither seek nor accept support from the teacher unions.

In the process the post-secondary enrollment option (PSEO) did pass. The program made it possible for 11th- and 12th-graders to enroll in college, earning credit toward high school and college graduation at the same time. At Perpich's insistence Bob Wedl and Jessie Montano got it implemented that fall. PSEO carried the essential idea of 'somebody else' offering public education in the community, foreshadowing what was to come next with chartering. Minnesota had begun broadening its state system of public education.

Concerned about being on the wrong side of the governor heading into the next legislative session, the MEA asked: Can't we make up? Perpich said: Sure. I'll create a discussion group. Bring whatever you want to this group; what it agrees on will be my program for '86.

At the initial meeting the education associations were surprised to see across the table people from all the groups that had worked with Perpich on open enrollment. After some grumbling about "What right do you have to be here?" the discussion became constructive. Verne Johnson said: We're not here to beat up on the past." Willard Baker, the school boards executive, responded: "I'm glad to hear you say that. We'll stipulate: We can do better."

"We'll stipulate: We can do better" said the school board executive

Bob Astrup launched into the 'I'm concerned' speech about choice. Verne took him on. "Bob, choice exists. You can send your child anywhere; move to another district or enroll in private school. It does take money.

But if you have money you have choice. Those who don't have money don't have choice. Some of us are trying to use public resources to offset those inequalities in private resources. That sounds to us like a liberal thing to do. Why are you against it? "

It was not easy. At one point Superintendent Don Bungum, the MASA president, interrupted, to say: "Don't talk about change". Around the table, silence. Finally: "For heaven's sake why not?" "To talk about change", Don said, "implies that what went before was not-OK."

Astrup was interesting. Dan Loritz had taught with him in Mounds View, and in March got us together for a long Saturday breakfast. At the end Bob sighed deeply and said, "Of course we do have the option to stonewall it". Yet in private moments he would describe the system as "torqued out", needing to shift into another gear.

The '86 session produced the option for students in one way or another 'not doing well' to attend nonprofit alternative schools contracted to districts. The Legislature also enacted the Area Learning Centers legislation making it possible to create alternative schools serving several districts. MAAP, the Minnesota Association of Alternative Programs, still operates.

Perpich persisted on inter-district open enrollment; finally getting it by 1988, staged in. The default arrangement was for the district to be open, requiring a board to vote affirmatively to close. Edina's decision to close to non-residents brought criticism to that upper-income district, helping reinforce the sense of choice as an effort at equity. PSI ran an ad about the opportunity: *"I didn't realize I could enroll my daughter in another public school district!"* Bill Salisbury at the Pioneer Press wrote that Perpich had 'struck gold' with the choice idea.

There had been a surprisingly positive report from the Gallup survey of national public opinion. A person there gave me the unpublished breakouts. These made it clear that support for choice was highest in low-income families where the parents had not graduated from high school; was strongest, in other words, among people who needed better schools most. Entirely logical. Politically significant. Those least favorable were those with the money to pay for their choices themselves.

Questions of equity and questions of ethics

Not surprisingly, quite logically, the discussion about choice was beginning to highlight long-standing—and for years too-little-discussed—questions about equity, fairness, in public education.

One dimension of that went clearly to the district system itself. We all understand how a metropolitan area has developed; with neighborhoods of different age and different value and with residences of like value grouped together. Lay down over a region like this a grid of picket-fences called school district boundaries and you have created a system stratified by income, social class and race. The re-equalization of school finance here in 1971 (see Chapter 10) had done much to equalize the financing. But the cities' changing demographics were creating ever-tougher challenges for the schools and their teachers.

A second dimension, set out in 1980 by Michael Lipsky, stems from the nature of the relationships between citizens and the public-service employees with whom they interact: especially teachers, police and social workers; relationships Lipsky described in **Street-Level Bureaucracy**. These are workers caught between the expectations of the public authority for which they work and the expectations and needs of the clients they are expected to serve. With time and resources limited, they must make quick decisions about the benefits to be provided and sanctions to be applied; doing their best to apply general rules to differing individual situations.

Inevitably their decisions affect people's life chances. The poorer the clients, Lipsky wrote, the more influence the bureaucrat has over them. Schools have long grouped students by perceived ability. John Goodlad, when he looked at schools: saw the least successful students being given the least able teachers and the lower-quality materials, and never catching up. Minneapolis for a time reported school by school the proportion of teachers with a master's degree and above, and the proportion of students eligible for free and reduced lunch. At the junior-high level the inverse correlation was perfect.

The policy discussion was bound to be difficult, where so great a difference existed between the rhetoric of 'children first' and the reality created by districting and by the arrangements for teachers and teaching. The questions about equity and ethics were to return later, in other forms.

The discussion begins to search for the 'different'

The support for 'choice' meant there needed to be more good schools for students to choose among. That meant thinking about what 'better' meant, and how to use all the good ideas stirring.

On a trip to Britain in 1986 I had a chance to learn about policy changes there. I got a full education from John Stevenson at the Association of County Councils, whom I'd met at Ditchley in '81, and from Stuart Maclure of the Times Education Supplement. The bill for local management of schools was then just going through Parliament. Polly Brown arranged a meeting with Keith Joseph, who asked if I knew about Alum Rock, and for some reason I can't recall I went into 10 Downing Street to talk with Brian Griffiths, the policy advisor.

In the summer of 1987 I wrote an article for the Harvard Business Review. It began: "Why is business so nice to the schools?" That bought me a letter from David Kearns, CEO at Xerox, later to be undersecretary of the U.S. Department. My article had quoted someone describing much business support as 'fuzzy altruism'. That brought a clip from the Omaha World-Herald reporting Warren Buffett's small grants to teachers. On it he'd written, "Just a little fuzzy altruism".

Ruth Anne Olson got a grant from Bill Linder-Scholer at Cray Research to help a group of math teachers do a business plan for a teacher partnership. The superintendent agreed their approach to teaching math would help, but asked: Will anyone get upset? Unable to assure him no one would get upset, the teachers folded their papers and went away.

"I've seen too many people who passed tests and failed life"

In early 1988 Perpich disappointed the Business Partnership about testing; told Loritz, "I've seen too many people who passed tests and failed life, and too many who failed tests and passed life. I'm not going to make testing that important."

In February Jeff Lapides from Baltimore came through; wanting to invest about $200 million of family money to create an education business; certain there must be opportunities. I told him I saw no way in. He wondered: How can this be? In July Donna Carter gave me an exit interview before leaving for a position in the private education world. She talked about the innovative technology school she'd created while superintendent in Robbinsdale: "Every month I watch it becoming more like every other school we have."

We kept looking for ways to facilitate change. I got Herb Morgenthaler to explain to teachers and others how Dayton's department stores operated as a mixture of owned and leased departments. That's when people thought: "We could organize a high school like that!"

Minnesota was not going to do vouchers. But on a visit here, Polly Williams, who'd gotten vouchers into Wisconsin law, proved a tough advocate; made it more difficult for Minnesotans not to do something. She had opposed David Bennett's busing Milwaukee students out to the suburbs. Turning through photos of school-bus accidents she kept asking, "Whose children are these? Look at the photos. Whose children are these?"

In '89 I left the Humphrey Institute. I was ready, and senior fellows were, anyway, not to be around indefinitely. It'd be good to be independent. I began the meetings of 'the Hamline group' that was to develop into Education|Evolving.

In '88, however, an idea first floated at the national level had produced a discussion in Minnesota that was to provide the agenda for all of us for the coming decade. The 'charter' idea.

CHAPTER 18:

Chartering: New Public Schools

Late in 1987 the Citizens League started a committee on school structure, chaired by John Rollwagen, a League active at Cray Research before becoming its CEO. The following April the committee noticed the reports of Albert Shanker's talk at the National Press Club, proposing teachers be allowed to start small schools, which—picking up the term from Ray Budde—he called 'charter' schools. The committee got the text, talked about the idea, and by September had a proposal almost finished.

In October the Minneapolis Foundation brought Shanker and Sy Fliegel, then with the community district schools in East Harlem, to its Itasca Seminar on Gull Lake. Shanker went over his proposal. He was leaving after lunch, and needing myself to get back to Minneapolis for my seminar, I offered him a ride to the airport. He accepted; we talked through the idea for three hours on the way down, getting to the airport 10 minutes before plane time, which you could do in those days. That evening, at Madden's, Joe Nathan, Senator Ember Reichgott, Rep. Ken Nelson and others began outlining a Minnesota initiative for chartering.

A month later the League issued its proposal for "Chartered Schools". It was actually not the first such. A year before, in Chicago, Joe Loftus had put a similar idea into that city's discussion, even using the term 'charter'. When Chicago went instead for 'parent-run schools' Joe put the proposal away. Few today know of Loftus' proposal.

In the 1989 session Senator Reichgott got chartering into the Senate omnibus bill. The House was not interested. But discussion continued about the essential idea of new and self-governed schools. That March I'd brought several persons from Britain here to explain their 'local management of schools': Christina Bienkowska, from the Department of Education and Science; Anne Sofer, soon to become chief education officer in the London borough of Tower Hamlets, and a headmaster from Cambridgeshire.

In December Marc Tucker asked me to join him and Mike Cohen in Albany for a discussion with the New York commissioner, Tom Sobol.

"That's a fertile idea for me".

New York was getting pressure to take over unsuccessful districts, as New Jersey had done. I mentioned the chartering idea. At the break Sobol walked over with his coffee cup and said, "That's a fertile idea for me". Clearly he did not want to become superintendent of a collection of the most difficult districts in New York state.

Again in the 1990 session Senator Reichgott got chartering into the Senate omnibus bill; again the House refused to accept it in conference. As the conference broke up, though, I heard Rep. Becky Kelso, a DFLer and former school board member in Shakopee, go over to Ember and say, "If you'd like to try that charter idea again next year, I'd like to help you". (Ember tells the whole story in **Zero Chance of Passage**, her definitive account of the origins of chartering.)

That summer I mailed-around a PSRP memo: "The States Will Have To Withdraw the Exclusive". The districting of the system is the heart of the problem, I wrote.

The boundaries create areas in which only a single organization is offering public education, to whose schools the students who live in that area are assigned. If a district does not offer better schools the state does not send in another organization that will: It accepts the pace at which the district is able or willing to move. The combination of mandatory attendance and the 'exclusive franchise' meant the state was assuring the districts their students, their revenues, almost everything important to their economic success...whether or not a district changed and improved and whether or not its students learned. The incentives were not aligned with the task the system had been given to perform. For a country serious about improvement that was an absurd arrangement. The state's job is not to run the schools, I wrote: It is to provide a workable system for those who do. *"Everywhere in this country the state is in default on that obligation."*

I mailed perhaps 300 copies of the memo. It seems to have gone viral through the Xerox machines. Several times I got a note asking for a clean copy; the writer saying, "The one I have has been copied so many times it won't copy any more."

Minnesota adopts chartering

Commissioner Randall returned to Nebraska. Governor Perpich named Tom Nelson to replace her. He asked Tom to rethink the bill for chartering. Tom brought the four communities of color into his task force. Most of the discussion was about what a school must do and must not do. Little was said about 'sponsors'—which was to be a problem later.

Discussions began, looking toward the '91 session. Ken Nelson wanted to support chartering but worried about the union reaction. At Ember's request Peter Vanderpoel and I went to see Betsy Rice, drafting the education bill. Her first reaction was traditional: These are not public schools. "They are part of the state's program of public education", we said. Betsy looked out the window for a time. "OK", she said.

That December Curt Johnson and I caught Arne Carlson, governor-elect, after a breakfast. He was abrupt: "We aren't going to do charter schools".

Early in the session Ember thought she had agreement that post-secondary institutions as well as districts could sponsor schools. But at a meeting with the Minnesota Federation of Teachers staff it was clear the state office had overruled her understanding with the Robbinsdale local. "This bill is going to pass the Senate", Ember said. The response was unspoken: We'll see about the House. She appealed to Shanker. He wrote back that he didn't get involved in local disputes.

Legislators were ready, though. There was quiet support in the background. One veteran DFL member of the Senate education committee said to me privately, "Nobody representing teachers has ever come to me to talk about education".

On the last day of the session the Senate chair passed by, saying about the conference committee: "We have five votes in Senate; two and a half in the House". Ken Nelson was the 'half'. He asked for amendments to provide a teacher-majority on the board of the school, to limit the number of schools to eight and to make the district the only sponsor. Reluctantly, Reichgott agreed. When a motion to recommit narrowly failed, chartering stayed in the omnibus bill; the schools to be known as "outcome-based schools". Governor Carlson signed. An opposition lobbyist growled: "We'll take care of this this summer".

Other states legislate

What followed surprised everybody.

The law was purely enabling legislation. It created no schools. Parents, teachers and others turned out to do the difficult work of creating schools. Joe Nathan organized early meetings; some among teachers. Soon Winona sponsored a Montessori school. Milo Cutter was the first to open a school, in Saint Paul. In the Department of Education Peggy Hunter was supportive.

As with the metropolitan legislation after 1967, it seemed important to build knowledge and interest elsewhere. I wrote memos passing around what I'd heard about activity in various states; about laws, schools and persons involved. Our strategy was always to get something to happen here in Minnesota; then talk about what had actually come into law. This is better than going around the country with an idea not implemented.

Early in '92, Jerry Hume invited me to meet with the California Business Roundtable. I went on from San Francisco to Sacramento, where Eric Premack had set up meetings with Gary Hart in the Senate, Delaine Eastin in the Assembly and others. The story of chartering's enactment there on the last night of the session—told in **Zero Chance of Passage**—is a classic in legislative process. Rochelle Stanfield called from the National Journal, interested in writing about chartering "even though it didn't pass in California". "It did pass in California", I said. Stunned silence.

Will Marshall had spotted the potential in public-school choice and chartering for the centrist program the Democratic Leadership Council was developing for Bill Clinton. He asked me to contribute to the 'education' chapter of the policy book he and Al From were preparing. I did that; noting that nothing prevents a president from laying proposals before the legislatures of the states, in whose law the K-12 system exists.

Something had sparked interest in Colorado. In January 1993 Barbara O'Brien at the Childrens Campaign called the first national meeting of those interested. Howard Fuller came, from Milwaukee. So did (California) Gary Hart; invited by Governor Romer to breakfast at the Brown Palace. It was a first chance also to discuss the idea directly with those in district public education.

In the summer of '93 the Graduate School of Education and the National Conference of State Legislatures co-hosted a session at Harvard, at the end of which Tim Van Wingen of the legislative staff handed me the bill to be considered in Michigan. In September the dean at Michigan State, Judy Lanier, brought all the education groups to a morning-long explanation of the charter idea. That evening, talking at the Radisson with his aide, Mike Addonizio, Governor Engler joined us.

In 1993 six states acted: Colorado, thanks to Romer and Rep. Peggy Kerns; Georgia, Michigan, Massachusetts, New Mexico and Wisconsin. Other states followed through the '90s as the discussion spread.

The astonishing national interest continued. In early '94 chartering was one of the 'threats' considered in a strategic planning process organized by the NEA (and I think never made public). The NEA sent me $300 for spending an icy February morning in Washington with the committee assigned to 'charter'. The '90s was the only time I ever earned preferred status on Northwest Airlines; making sometimes two trips a week. I saw state capitals I never thought I'd see: Santa Fe, Baton Rouge (where they show you the bullet-hole), Concord, Springfield, Harrisburg (magnificent building from Pennsylvania's heyday), Olympia, Columbus, Topeka (a chance to visit Central High school where the *Brown* case began), Providence, Boise, Oklahoma City, Honolulu. Eric Premack and I had a fascinating meeting at the Tyson's headquarters where Stewart Springfield, heading the early Walton Foundation, got together all the Arkansas groups, including three of the sharpest legislators I ever met. The idea was getting around.

Everywhere it was a 'state capitol policy initiative'. Sometimes the successful authors were freshmen: Joe Tedder in Florida; Jim Rubens in New Hampshire; Bob Perls in New Mexico. In New Jersey Tom Corcoran was working with Joe Doria and Jack Ewing, two old pros. In Delaware, Dave Sokola, whom I had not met. It was strikingly bipartisan. Sometimes staff helped discreetly in the background; as, Mary Young in the Pennsylvania Senate.

Everywhere it was a 'state capitol policy initiative'

The idea sold itself. There was no national organization, with local chapters. No financing. State leadership was simply ready; saw immediately that if the districts were not giving them what they wanted it was fully within their power to "get somebody else who will". There were citizen initiatives on laws and on schools. Sue Hollins in New Hampshire, Laura Friedman in Missouri, Dick Meinhard in Oregon.

Its spread confounded the 'realists', not accustomed to seeing a radical idea succeed against the opposition of the interest groups. The capitol reporter for the Chicago Tribune was emphatic: "Not in Illinois!" Yet a version did pass in Illinois.

The stories would make great case material for a student of legislative process: Minnesota, of course; Gary Hart on the last night of the session in California; Governor Romer, going into the House Democratic caucus in Colorado; Mike Fox in Ohio; in Pennsylvania, Dwight

Evans bringing over the Philadelphia Black delegation late at night for Governor Ridge's bill. I've always considered it a great credit to the state legislature as an institution. New York is an exception: the Wall Street Journal was right about its legislature "not passing this public-interest legislation until bribed to do so"; Governor Pataki holding hostage the legislators' pay increase.

Some states passed weak laws intended not to work or to get the issue off the agenda: mainly sparsely-settled states in the Great Plains and rural New England, states in the deep South and Appalachia. Washington state was logical for chartering, but never could get its thinking straight.

Washington D.C. was a special case. Dale MacIver, Congressman Fraser's former aide, pointed out Section 601 of the Home Rule Act in which Congress reserved the right as legislature for the District to act at any time on any matter. Jon Schnur, with Secretary Riley, Jim Ford, with the D.C. City Council and Ted Rebarber with Congressman Gunderson worked out the plan that had Mayor Barry appointing the members of the new charter public school board *from a list provided by the Secretary of Education*. Put only good names on the list and the mayor couldn't screw it up. Jo Baker became the chair (later its executive director).

The charter sector spreads and evolves

Chartering was popular immediately with parents. Education writers gave the schools good coverage. The idea clearly tapped into a powerful desire for 'different'.

Minnesota quickly began to improve its law; adding an appeal to the state board; raising and later removing the cap on the number of schools allowed; adding post-secondary institutions and later large nonprofits as sponsors; providing lease aid.

Elsewhere there were variations. Betsy Rice's language was visible in several early laws, but soon new and non-Minnesota features were appearing. Missouri's program opened chartering just in St. Louis and

Unfortunately, 'charter' became an adjective

Kansas City. In Michigan and Arizona charters could go directly to commercial organizations. Arizona created a state-wide alternate sponsor. Wisconsin did a different law just for Milwaukee.

The nomenclature changed—unfortunately. Minnesota initially called its schools 'outcome-based'. Ohio called them 'Community Schools'. But quickly and soon universally everyone began to say, "charter schools". Making 'charter' an adjective was to have profound consequences, making it seem unnecessary to see what in fact the schools were pedagogically; encouraging people to believe that structural change itself had learning effects, obscuring chartering as a strategy for innovation.

It was fascinating to watch others in education policy react. As Will Marshall had sensed it would, 'charter' was proving more appealing politically than 'voucher'. Voucher groups (warily) approved, perhaps because chartering extended choice, but continued their effort. The Edison Project, on its way to developing private schools, shifted quickly into the chartered sector.

I was asked to a meeting at the Hoover Institution at Stanford, at which Milton Friedman complained about "my fellow intellectuals, like Professor Coons" (in reference to Jack's opposition to the Alibrandi voucher initiative in California) "making the perfect the enemy of the good". I drifted over to read the name-tag of a quiet, white-haired African-American participant. Eldridge Cleaver.

Policy shops began to pay attention. Groups in the district sector remained generally opposed, but soon after its passage in Colorado the executive of the school boards association, Randy Quinn, was suggesting to members that this might be "a blessing in disguise". I called to ask about his change of mind. "I began to see it during the legislative debate", he said.

Here and there a teacher union would start a school to show it was open-minded, or perhaps to show that 'charter' and unionization could be made compatible. University schools of public affairs came into education policy. At Minnesota and elsewhere it was easy, but at Harvard it took a struggle with the Graduate School of Education for the Kennedy School to get into the field. Foundations begin to pick up on the idea: Walton; Gates. The New Schools Venture Fund was formed to encourage 'entrepreneurs' into education; into the chartered sector.

Back in Minnesota, Jon Schroeder started the Charter Friends National Network (CFNN) to connect the state charter groups. We had lunch at the airport with the Challenge Foundation; John Bryan on his way home to Oregon and B.J. Steinbrook who flew up from Texas. With their help the CFNN continued for about seven years. We did a model bill and a memo explaining the financing arrangement. Happily, Jeanne Allen at the Center for Education Reform soon took over tracking the laws and schools.

The national government helps

President Clinton, thanks to Will Marshall's urging, became (and remained) a good supporter of chartering. Secretary Riley visited Minnesota early; Jon Schnur with him. Clinton maintained his support despite pressure. In the final year of his term he flew to Minnesota again to visit Milo Cutter's City Academy. In the lobby of the Saint Paul Hotel some of those who'd flown out with him told me that on the way the president of the American Federation of Teachers (AFT) was still phoning Air Force One, trying to discourage the visit.

In 1994 Senator Durenberger proposed the federal government help financially with the start-up of schools. A $650,000 program was approved. Mike Smith, undersecretary, was important in getting Congress to accept the principle of deferring to state law on the questions of who could authorize schools and who could operate schools. The U.S. Department began hosting the early national charter meetings.

In 2000 the Ford Foundation/Kennedy School 'Innovations' award was given to Minnesota for its chartering law. Twice earlier, in 1997 and 1998, Governor Carlson had applied and been rejected. So when the circular soliciting applications came again in 1999 I wrote Susan Berresford, the president. Your foundation, I said, is representing as a competition for innovation *in American government* what it is operating as a competition for innovation *in American public administration*. Soon after, with so many states having enacted chartering, Minnesota began to get hints: Do apply again. Minnesota did, and this time won one of the $100,000 awards for its law.

Despite the significant national attention, chartering was not fully established. Opposition, controversy and misunderstanding were affecting the discussion in major ways. A lot more work was needed. For that we had to create a 'setting' where we could gather some people and do a good deal of thinking.

That became Education|Evolving. Let's consider it next; that will take us into the issues-in-controversy.

CHAPTER 19:

Education|Evolving
As a 'Setting'

Out of the Bailey Room group we gradually created a design shop that we came to say was defined mainly by what it was not: not governmental, not academic, not commercial, not partisan. Not even a real organization; a collection of individuals. Some DFL and some Republican; experienced variously in K-12 education, in general government, in politics, in consulting, in the nonprofit world. Some in Minnesota, some elsewhere; some full-time, some part-time; some paid, some unpaid. All with a sense of the way systems, structure and incentives matter. We had financial help while Bruno Manno was at the Annie Casey Foundation; after that from resources to which I had access. This made the group a 'setting' for redesign, with the time and the freedom to explore ideas outside the conventional.

Dan Loritz was part of it. Verne Johnson, for a time. Jon Schroeder, after returning from Washington. Joe, after becoming dean of the Hamline graduate school of education. Later: Susan Heegaard, Stacy Becker, Kim Farris, Ed Dirkswager, Curt Johnson, John Boland, others. Bob Wedl, after leaving the state, where he'd been commissioner.

Wanting a name, we settled on Education|Evolving (E|E). It was 'virtual'; no staff, no office, no mission statement, no organizational complications. Lars Johnson built a website while still in college. (After it formalized he was to be its executive director.) It was in a way the old Citizens League model: getting to understand the system, talking with people involved, listening, working to come up with proposals designed to be both imaginative and realistic. We had a long afternoon in 1999 with Jack Frymier about student motivation. Sessions with Howard Fuller, Anne Bryant. After 2002 I was regularly at the New Schools Venture Fund 'summits'. Joe Graba began to attend the meetings of TURN, the Teacher Union Reform Network. We tried both to explain and to persuade: legislators, foundations, others in education policy.

The sense was strong in the group of the need for the chartered sector to produce innovation. Joe saw the central challenge clearly: "Almost everybody wants schools to be better; almost nobody wants them to be different".

The national strategy adopted about 1990 in No Child Left Behind had in fact rested on the notion that education could be better *without* the schools having to be different. After the Risk report in 1983 there had been a brief interest in 'restructuring'. But no clear idea appeared of what that would mean. No one saw any way to 'change everything'. So in 1990 the practical conclusion seemed obvious: We aren't going to change the system we have; let's accept that, and work to get its schools to perform better. How? Set standards for student learning, test to see if schools have met those standards, impose consequences if they have not. The 'accountability model'.

Fairly quickly our effort to stress innovation brought us into disagreement with the way the chartered sector was developing nationally.

Seeing chartering as a strategy for change

For the first 10 years the new chartered sector was diffuse, indifferently organized, not well financed. Schools were mostly single-unit, freestanding entities. The state organizations were associations of schools, loosely linked through the Charter Friends National Network.

By 2002 chartering was in law in some form in most of the major states of America; a sense of its potential developing. Predictably, people began to think about creating a national organization. The early idea was for its board to be a mixture of state association people and others selected by those from the state associations. Howard Fuller agreed to be chair. Dean Millot was hired from RAND to be its executive.

The foundations by now interested in the sector, and increasingly turned-to for financial support, were reluctant. Their preference for a 'leadership organization' rather than a membership organization cystallized at a meeting at Charlottesville, VA in 2003. It is time for "the little people" to step aside, one consultant said privately, "and for the heavy hitters to take over".

The initial design for a National Charter Schools Alliance was aborted, replaced a year later by the National Association of Public Charter Schools. Nelson Smith was brought in to be its executive. In 2005 he assembled the charter family at Mackinac Island where he laid out the new mission. Though not put quite this way, the idea was to suggest that chartering could do what district schools could not. That is, produce schools that get elementary students in the cities to score well on state tests and close schools that do not. The charter sector would grow by doing traditional school better, demonstrating accountability for achievement conventionally defined.

After that, the group of large foundations moved to create and support entities working to implement the new strategy; schools and support organizations, state and national. The National Association of Charter School Authorizers (NACSA) appeared, to set standards enforcing accountability for 'performance'. 'Scaling up' became the mantra. The New Schools Venture Fund was focusing on creating 'entrepreneurs' and promoting charter management organizations (CMOs) as the way to spread 'quality schools'. There was a Charter Schools Growth Fund. A succession of persons from these organizations moved into the U.S. Department of Education.

Working to develop what we felt was the original concept of chartering, Education|Evolving found itself now engaged in a difficult discussion. Others in the charter family asked if we didn't believe in accountability. We said we were fine with accountability, but asked: Accountability for what? For achievement, certainly. What achievement? English language and math only? Assessment only to measure proficiency on the state exams?

Researchers as well as the media seemed to have fallen in with the notion that school success, school quality, was to be identified only by student mean proficiency scores. This was indefensible intellectually, as Stephen Raudenbush explained in his Angoff Lecture to the Educational Testing Service in 2004. But that narrow concept of achievement seemed impossible to shake.

Worse, people began talking not about 'chartered' schools but about 'charter schools'. Making 'charter' an adjective suggested the new schools were a kind of school. If so, then surely they could be compared with other kinds of schools. Quickly proponents and opponents undertook 'research' to show that 'charter schools' did or did not 'perform better' than district schools. This was bizarre: Research might equally have compared scores in south-facing schools and east-facing schools.

The essence of chartering was to permit the organizers to create whatever kind of school they wished; it was in effect an R&D program for public education. The failure to look first to see what the schools chartered were as schools—what they had their students reading, seeing, hearing and doing—was an embarrassment to education research. But the comparisons became the game. "Everybody expects it" John Merrow wrote in an email.

A schism was developing in chartering. Chartering had been a reformation in the church of public education. In the reformation 500 years ago the 'protestants' had quickly split into sects. So also with chartering. Different strategies, concepts, were emerging about the purpose and role of the new second sector of public education. The National Alliance speaks only of 'charter schools' and 'high-performing charter schools', perhaps feeling the distinction between conventional schools and innovative schools would is too complicated for the policy thinking in Washington. Today it particularly stresses the popularity of 'charter schools' in communities of color. The Alliance is now much better skilled at defending the sector. This helps, in the counter-reformation being conducted against chartering.

Continuing to question conventional thinking

We found ourselves increasingly dissenters from the national consensus ... realized we were drifting beyond what Ed Dirkswager called "the standard-enlightened" view of public education; beyond both the generally accepted 'givens' of the district system and of the process by which school and system change.

At a Wallace Funds meeting in Colorado I suggested to Gordon Ambach, then heading the Council of Chief State School Officers: "The notion that there can be only one organization offering public education in a city *no matter how large* is absurd on its face". He had not thought about things quite that way.

In May 2004 Joe Graba raised the basic questions about purpose and strategy in a meeting of foundations in Denver; the first-ever collaboration, we were told, between the Council on Foundations and the Philanthropy Roundtable. Joe stated his and E|E's conviction about the need for different schools, created new: "We cannot get the schools we need by changing the schools we have." This connected with the proposal the commission staffed by Paul Hill had made to the Education Commission of the States (ECS) a year or so earlier for districts to have both owned and contracted schools.

That December Chris Cross asked Joe to do the major evening talk to The Cleveland Conference. Joe talked candidly and persuasively about how difficult the journey had been for him, from where he started as a teacher and union active and DFL legislator, to the conclusion that schools needed to be created new and needed to be "radically different".

We had made contact in October 2001 with Clayton Christensen at Harvard Business School; had brought him by video into our national meeting at Hamline to explain his concept of 'disruptive innovation'.

In July 2005 Ted Sanders, then heading ECS, put Christensen on the agenda at its annual meeting, in Denver. Curt Johnson, Joe Graba and I watched the reaction in that group to his 'disruptive innovation' analysis. Soon after—through Curt—E|E was in the collaboration with Clay that in 2008 produced his bestselling application of the idea to education: **Disrupting Class.**

It was good to be challenging what others took as given. The discussion was dominated by people themselves successful in school, as were their children. Not surprisingly they tended to feel school and system are fine; that the problems must lie with the students and their families. This cried out for challenge.

We found ourselves dissenting from more and more of the concepts of 'real school'—from its notions of age-grading, of 'batch processing' in courses and classes; from its concepts of achievement and measurement. We found ourselves challenging the concept of adults 'delivering education' to young people. And questioning the assumption, which seemed implicit in the strategy of 'standards', that students will learn if told they must learn.

We were increasingly concerned about the growing orthodoxy that standards would be sufficient to drive change, about the insistence that only the state assessments mattered as a measure of success, and about the one-dimensional definition of success for student and school.

Normally, judgments about success and quality are multi-dimensional, we said. Think about your job, your neighborhood, your house, your church; for that matter, about people you know. Think about your car: There is more than original cost. There is also design and color and comfort and safety and capacity—and resale value. All these go into your decision about quality, do they not? Judgments are made on-balance, are they not? So why not judgments-on-balance for student learning and for schools?

We began to feel the narrow concept of 'achievement' discriminated against young people not from middle-class backgrounds; seemed not to acknowledge or respect skills and knowledge other than English and math. Bob Wedl tellingly asked: If a reasonable facility with two or more languages were a measure of achievement, which students in your community would be the high-achieving?

We were dissenting also from conventional concepts of the strategy for change: from the notion that it was essential to be 'comprehensive', 'systemic', with all elements aligned. "You have to have a fully-worked-out plan", one leading academic told us. Outside, afterward, Graba and I looked at each other in disbelief: Nothing in our experience suggested that is the way legislatures work.

We were inclined to question, too, the conclusion that no major change is possible; that 'reform' can do no more than improve incrementally the schools we have. That was a reasonable conclusion from the time when there was no way to create public schools new. But now it had become possible—through chartering—to create new and different public schools; autonomous schools on contract to a district or to some other authorizer. We wanted to develop that potential.

The goal: to innovate with teaching and learning

All this was pushing us to think more deeply about the strategy of change; about the importance of the 'different'. We knew we stood outside the consensus, but after the experience with chartering it was not easy to persuade our group that unconventional ideas cannot succeed.

The idea emerging was to develop an open sector, in which improvement and innovation would run in parallel. In February '08 Education|Evolving sent around a paper titled, "The Other Half of the Strategy", arguing for creating different schools as well as improving the existing. In 2010 Education|Evolving circulated "It's Time To Get Beyond Traditional School".

Our group was talking more and more about a strategy that:

- to produce success for a school *might require different governance* for the school. This revived our thinking in the '80s about school-based decision-making and teacher professional partnerships.

- to produce success for students *might require different approaches to learning*; an alternative both to the default arrangement of whole-class instruction and to the notion of adults 'delivering education' to children.

- to satisfy the expectations for performance and accountability *might require a broader concept of achievement*; of what young people know and can do.

- to be implemented, might require *a new concept of system change.*

- to produce change in K-12 generally might require *a successful charter sector stimulating the district sector.*

We were increasingly persuaded of the importance of autonomy for schools in the charter sector. Over and over we heard their teachers and administrators say: If we find a problem we can fix it ourselves; have the problem fixed tomorrow. We began to be interested in this idea of autonomy applied to the district sector, the proposal from Paul Hill for a 'portfolio' of schools on contract. And we were impressed by the success of the schools in which teachers organized on the model of a professional partnership; a striking departure from the accepted wisdom that schools had to be organized on the bureau, the boss/worker, model.

Also, the process for chartering schools needed to change. In the initial debate too little attention had been given to the 'sponsor' (later, 'authorizer'). Joe Graba and I got together six local sponsors. They'd never met or talked. They liked the interchange, and soon there was a sponsors' network, financed initially by the state department.

Minnesota law at the time let organizations in some category of 'eligible' declare themselves sponsors. All were organizations that had something bigger and more important to do: run a district, operate a college, manage a large nonprofit. We began to suggest the state make available nonprofits that could devote their entire attention to chartering; requesting proposals, reviewing proposals, deciding on proposals and overseeing the schools they approved. In 2009, with Commissioner Seagren's support, the 'single-purpose authorizer' came into law; three initially to be available.

One more vine across the river.

We kept thinking about what Jack Frymier had said: that any successful effort to improve learning will begin by improving student motivation. That got us interested in personalizing learning. Carol McFarlane made us aware of a teacher who had individualized his third-grade classroom. Bob Wedl and I visited Mr. Pai. He cooperated on a small video (see www.educationevolving.org/pai), an interesting personal story and an important pedagogical and policy story. Level Up Academy later brought this model into a new (chartered) elementary in White Bear Lake.

The interest in personalizing learning further encouraged our thinking about the professional role for teachers. 'Good teaching' was beginning, nationally, to seem more important to learning than 'standards', so interest was building in what was loosely called 'teacher leadership'.

In September 2008 we had brought people to Saint Paul—union folks, teachers in partnerships, Richard Ingersoll from the school of education at Penn and Joe Aguerreberre, then heading the National Board of Professional Teaching Standards—for a discussion about this idea. Leaving, Joe said to me: "We've always seen site-management, the teachers' push to be in charge of learning, as a power struggle. The possibility that it is a route to better learning is a whole new idea for us."

Thinking about that idea, and about what might result, we began to see some larger implications. More and more we began to think that professionalizing teaching might perhaps be the 'how' for system change.

CHAPTER 20:

The Teacher-Partnership Idea

Chartering had brought the opportunity to try this idea of professionalism for teachers.

Ruth Anne Olson had gotten us to think of professionalism as being able to say, "Tell me what you want done. Don't tell me how to do it: I'm a professional: I know *how* to do it." We'd had that evening discussion in 1982 (See page 171) about the different relationships between professionals and administrators in law and medicine, and had seen the interest this idea aroused in teachers. Still, though, teachers were not allowed professional status. 'Professional issues' were reserved to management.

Minnesota's chartering law said a school could organize as a nonprofit or as a cooperative. The people starting Minnesota New Country School in Le Sueur inquired about this. We met one afternoon at the Sheraton-Midway in Saint Paul. Dick Fitzgerald was there; the law partner who had been in the 1982 conversation. So was Dan Mott, who'd been legislative aide to the chair of the Senate K-12 Finance Committee when in law school, now practicing in the area of co-op law. Dan advised forming New Country as a nonprofit but suggested forming a cooperative as well, as a vehicle for the teachers. I said that if they'd work with Dan, I'd pay half his bill. And they did.

From the start their (workers) cooperative seemed successful. The school itself was a nonprofit with no employees. Its board had only contracts: for space, for lunch, with the district for transportation and extracurriculars, and with EdVisions, the teacher co-operative, for the operation of the school. The teachers wanted to handle both the non-traditional learning program they were creating and the administration of it. That worked, and in a few years the school moved to a new building in Henderson.

Early in 2000 Midge and I were in Seattle on vacation. Barbara O'Brien had arranged for me to see Tom Vander Ark, newly in charge of education for the Gates Foundation. I showed Tom photos taken inside New Country — described by someone as "a messy Kinko's". "Is this a high school?" Yes. "Is it a charter school?" Yes. A few weeks later Tom and Tony Wagner from Harvard visited Henderson. Tom made EdVisions the first of several grants to replicate its cooperative and its project-based learning.

We watched New Country—which soon was getting as many as 500 visitors a year. We went to Ed Dirkswager about editing a book to encourage the partnership idea. After leaving state service (where he had been Minnesota's commissioner of human services) Ed had gone into the hospital field; later consulted with physician partnerships. Various of us contributed chapters. It was published in 2002, titled **Teachers As Owners.**

Ed and Kim Farris-Berg looked at the most fully teacher-influenced schools they could identify; in 2012 wrote up their findings in **Trusting Teachers with School Success.** Schools in which teachers are empowered—collegially—with professional roles; are able, for example, to personalize learning in order to motivate students. Teachers recognize: It's the students who will make the school successful.

Teachers, and unions, become intrigued

Traditionally in public education the big decisions about teachers' roles and about professional issues—what's taught and how it's taught—had been made outside the school, by district boards and the central office. "We're the ones who run the schools", board members say.

Unions have tried at times to make professional issues a subject of bargaining, but have not been able to win that for their members either through negotiation or through legislation. In 1998 the Minnesota School Boards Association asked those seeking the DFL nomination for governor about this. All five hedged. Afterward, Bob Meeks, MSBA executive director, told his group: The control of professional issues is the last real authority boards have. If we lose that we have nothing.

Denied professional role and status, teachers react predictably. "We argue about salaries and benefits and working conditions because that's all you let us argue about", Gene Mammenga said to me once, when lobbyist for the MEA.

As professional roles began to appear for teachers in the chartered sector, district teachers and their unions began to be interested.

In 2003 Deborah Wadsworth at Public Agenda agreed to ask, in their periodic survey of how teachers feel about their life and work, a new question: "How interested would you be in working in a charter school run and managed by teachers themselves?" This asked teachers to affirm an interest in the charter sector before they could reach the question of teachers being in charge. Still, 58 per cent of those questioned in that survey, conducted by Yankelovich, said they would be somewhat or very interested; two-thirds of the under-five-year teachers and half the over-20-year teachers. Those numbers effectively disposed of the 'Would anyone want to do it?' question.

A veteran union-active teacher in Milwaukee, Cris Parr, was among those visiting New Country School (see page 199). With help from her father, John, earlier head of AFSCME in Milwaukee, Cris started a teacher-cooperative school there. With the support of then-superintendent Bill Andrekopoulos, about a dozen more appeared in Milwaukee;

teachers negotiating waivers from the master agreement involving especially professional evaluation and the use of day, week and year.

In Minnesota the interest was initially an extension of Louise Sundin's long support for professionalism while president of the Minneapolis Federation of Teachers (MFT) and on the executive committee of the AFT. Louise had become convinced that if there are ever going to be schools that offer teachers truly professional roles, teachers will have to create them.

In 2005 the MFT had supported legislation for site-based schools. Finding the district reluctant to delegate autonomy, the MFT returned in 2009 for the 'self-governed schools' legislation that wrote the key autonomies into the law. This converted the decision into a simple 'We will' or 'No, we won't'.

When that, too, aroused no district interest, union people began to look at the chartered sector. Some from elsewhere visited Minnesota; some from Milwaukee. Marc Tucker connected us with John Wilson, then executive director of the NEA. In 2011 Louise and others in the leadership of the MFT created one of the new nonprofits (see page 195) able to authorize new schools in Minnesota's charter sector; the Minnesota Guild of Public Charter Schools. It became the first and probably remains today the only such in America.

Louise Sundin had gotten Joe Graba into meetings of the Teacher Union Reform Network (TURN) There he was finding interest growing as the pressures for accountability came down on teachers and unions. Teacher union leadership was understandably apprehensive about the conventional 'reform' agenda. But their impulse to resist testing was causing them to be seen as resisting accountability, and as defending the private interest of their members rather than advancing the public and student interest.

We began to articulate what we saw as their way out.

The old deal had been that, not controlling professional issues, teachers would not be accountable for student learning. Now the deal was changing: Teachers were to be accountable for student learning *even though management would still control professional issues.* We thought most people would consider that unfair.

Joe's advice, though, was: Don't fight accountability. Leverage off its pressure, to get teachers into professional roles. Say: If boards and superintendents are going to decide what's taught and how it's taught, then boards and superintendents should be accountable. If teachers are to be accountable for student and school success then teachers should be able to control what matters for success.

Moving the idea nationally

In the discussion developing about 'teacher leadership' the partnership model was (is still) the clearest and boldest. Most of that discussion is about enlarging teacher roles within the standard boss/worker model. Education|Evolving proposes 'flipping the pyramid' so the professionals are truly in charge of a school, a department, a grade-level or program, in a district or perhaps across districts.

Richard Ingersoll, at Penn, became interested. His well-received book in 2003, **Who Controls Teachers' Work?** had concluded that whoever it is, it isn't teachers. I'd called, said: "Are you aware there are schools in this country in which teachers do fully control their own work?" He said, "No, tell me about that." That began a close and productive relationship.

Richard has discovered generally in his research that schools work better where teacher roles are larger. His research has established a correlation between student achievement—though conventionally defined, and the result of teachers' influence simply *over the 'rules' and the culture of the schools*. He now follows closely the ways 'teacher-powered' schools are changing the approach to student learning.

In April 2010 Secretary Duncan's liaison to teachers and unions, Jo Anderson, arranged for Carrie Bakken from Avalon School and Brenda Martinez from ALAS in Milwaukee to explain to Duncan and his top staff how in the partnership arrangement they make decisions, arrange the learning, manage the school and its finances and select, evaluate, compensate and when necessary terminate teachers.

In October 2012 when TURN met in Minneapolis Louise Sundin brought in teachers from Avalon to explain how its teachers work when fully in charge. Graba then advised Education|Evolving the partnership idea was ready to go national.

The following summer, in Washington for Marc Tucker's event, I talked with Scott Widmeyer. We retained his firm to develop a national initiative. Focus groups and surveys showed support for what we came to call the 'teacher-powered' arrangement at 70 per cent and above, both among teachers and with the general public. In 2014 Education|Evolving partnered with the Center for Teaching Quality on an effort to build awareness of, interest in, support for and use of the partnership idea. Go to www.teacherpowered.org to see that initiative, led now by Education|Evolving; Lars Esdal and Amy Junge from her office in southern California.

I reprinted the notes from the 1982 discussion about "doctors, lawyers and teachers" (see page 171); sent them to persons in the developing discussion and found they made a considerable impression. Flying to Washington from Omaha where she lives, Maddie Fennell, assigned to 'teacher leadership' for Secretary Duncan, read the packet. "My mind was reeling", she wrote me that evening.

Lars, Amy and Alex Vitrella organized a first national conference around this idea in November 2015. About 220 teachers from 23 states came to Minneapolis to spend a weekend talking about how to secure the 'teacher-powered' arrangement and how to operate it once they had it. Half were from chartered schools; half from schools in the district sector. A website appeared: http://www.teacherpowered.org.

At the second national meeting, in Los Angeles in January 2017, the group was larger, with a higher proportion of teachers from the unionized district sector. A third meeting, in Boston in the Fall of 2018, was larger still. And EE arranged an interesting side-meeting: It included the director of strategy for the NEA, the executive vice president of the AFT, Peggy Brookins, president of the National Board of Professional Teaching Standards, Richard Ingersoll, people from the Boston Teachers Union and others. In the fall of 2020 the fourth national meeting, held remotely of course, doubled the Boston attendance, with over 600 teachers paying to participate.

In April 2021 Curt Johnson published the history, the shape of the movement, its essential argument and, persuasively, its prospects in **A New Deal for Teachers.**

Districts begin to give teachers 'agency' to change

We were slow to pick up on a parallel development in the local district sector. Even before the idea of the teacher-powered school the idea of greater teacher autonomy and more-personalized learning had begun to develop in Spring Lake Park where Don Helmstetter had become the superintendent and in Farmington where Jay Haugen had been hired in 2009.

What has developed is an ingenious variation on the essential idea. Teachers are simply told that, to graduate young people with the knowledge, skills and personal characteristics the board wants, they are free and encouraged to change the way they work with students in any way they wish *if they wish*. Nothing is required; no one *has* to change anything. Failure is OK: What is important is to try things.

Both districts are now in their second generation of leadership; Haugen having been succeeded by Jason Berg (earlier the high school principal) and Helmstetter by Jeff Ronneberg (an elementary principal in Spring Lake Park when Helmstetter was superintendent). In 2020 Charles Kyte interviewed teachers and administrators in the two districts, from elementary school to central office; asking how they responded and saw others responding. In his report they pretty much speak for themselves. See https://bit.ly/kytereportandappendix.

Jay Haugen moved to EdVisions, the nonprofit created to spread the teacher-cooperative and project-based-learning model at New Country School. He has set out to spread the model to other districts in Minnesota.

Seeing the importance of 'encouraging innovation'

This picks up the old wisdom about motivating those at the working level.

Chester Barnard set out the rationale in **The Functions of the Executive** in 1938. The book became a classic in business management (and among political scientists for its observation that *authority resides in the party to whom an order is given)*. That captured Barnard's central message, that in an organization success depends on the leader's ability to elicit cooperation from others. Similarly, Deborah Wadsworth, when heading Public Agenda, quoted Daniel Yankelovich's observation: There's a level of effort people will give you to keep their job; There's another level they will give you if motivated to do so. Your job in managing an organization, or in designing an organization, is to elicit that level of discretionary effort.

In 2014, killing time in our airport bookstore on my way to Nashville for the national meeting, of the Education Writers Association, I picked up Paul Kennedy's **Engineers of Victory**. It is an account of the innovation and problem-solving that won World War II. Roosevelt and Churchill at their meeting in Casablanca in early 1943 had set the strategy: to supply Britain across the Atlantic, to bomb Germany night and day, to open a second front in France. But no one knew how to defeat the German U-boats, how to protect the bombers over Berlin or how to land an army on a hostile defended shore. These and other problems were solved—in about 18 months—by people 'on the front lines' given the freedom to try things. Their story shapes Kennedy's essential lesson: Success comes when those in charge create "a climate of encouragement for innovation", stimulating problem-solvers at all levels in the organization to tackle large and apparently intractable problems.

It was impossible not to take these lessons into the education policy discussion; impossible not to wonder what schools and teachers — and students, surely important co-workers on the job of learning—might do were such a "climate of encouragement for innovation" created for them.

The ideas were beginning to come together, into a simple—obvious—strategy for turning public education into a self-improving system.

CHAPTER 21:

Trying To Think Out the How

By the end of the '90s the discussion about chartering had slowed, nationally as well as in Minnesota. Interest turned increasingly to the larger questions about how to use it for innovation. This saw Education|Evolving organizing meetings, local and national, in the Twin Cities area and on the coasts, east and west, trying to think through ways the 'open sector' strategy could produce major system change.

There were the meetings involving Clayton Christensen at Harvard Business School (See page 193) and Joe Graba's session in 2004 with the foundations and his presentation in 2005 to The Cleveland Conference (See page 193).

There were several focused on the partnership or workers cooperative as an innovation for teachers. In late 2003 Joe took Cris Parr to Washington, to a meeting organized by Will Marshall at the Progressive Policy Institute. Cris, a teacher from Milwaukee, the NEA's largest district, did a morning session with the AFT at which none of the probing questions could find anything not to like about the idea. In 2010 came the session with Secretary Duncan and his top people (See page 103).

We made a real effort to reach influential organizations and individuals. We did a major meeting at Wingspread on strategy in April

2007. Rick Hess hosted a meeting for us at the American Enterprise Institute in Washington. Tony Bryk, by then at the Carnegie Institute for the Advancement of Teaching, hosted one on the potential for learning technology in the open sector. Mike Smith was helpful while heading education for the Hewlett Foundation. The annual sessions of the New Schools Venture Fund were a learning experience; provided valuable contacts.

In 2011 the Education Commission of the States recognized chartering as a major contribution to American education; Dan Loritz and I went to Denver for that presentation. It is striking how often the Conant Award has gone to people not themselves educators: to several governors and other policymakers and—deservedly—to Ron Wolk, the founding editor of Education Week, with whom we had a long and productive relationship.

In 2009 I must have gone to four national meetings on innovation. In Boston, Jobs for the Future had trouble as it tried to focus on personalizing learning. Asked to apply that idea attendees said: "It's all I can do to manage my class of 25 students. Now you want me to work with each student individually? I don't get it." I kicked myself for not having brought along the photo showing students at New Country School working on their projects. I sent it afterward to Richard Kazis, who used it in the conference report. That picture has since gone all over America.

In 2000 Finland had become famous when its students topped the world rankings on the PISA assessment. We learned much from talking with Pasi Sahlberg, the leading explainer of Finnish education, who came here in 2011. In August 2012 he got me into the American delegation visiting Finland. Discovering that in Finland public education is a function of general city government—along with public works, public safety, public parks, etc.—put an important new perspective on its implications for education here.

By this time my own role was changing. Lars Esdal joined the Labrador Foundation in June 2014, became its president two years later and soon became executive director of Education|Evolving. I again began again to operate more independently.

I went to education meetings of the Philanthropy Roundtable, in Philadelphia, Chicago, Boston and Indianapolis; found them focused on doing conventional school better; essentially the 'improvement' strategy.

Out of what we'd learned in all the discussions and meetings I began writing what became a series of books. The first appeared in 2004: **Creating the Capacity for Change—How and Why Governors and Legislatures Are Opening a New-Schools Sector in Public Education.** It was mainly an analysis of the system's difficulty with change. It opened with the assertion: "The current theory of action contains a critical flaw"—meaning, the commitment to work within the givens of the traditional system. Everything later built off that understanding.

In 2014 and 2016 I wrote two small books both arguing the strategy of innovation and improvement. **The Split-Screen Strategy** opened with the story of Paul MacCready, who with his *Gossamer* aircraft had won the prizes for human-powered flight at which conventional aircraft structural designers had failed. "Little in our schools and culture forces us to get away from established patterns and to look at things in different ways", he had written. "We need to be skeptical and try different routes to solve problems."

In 2017 in **Thinking Out the How** I set the story of our developing education policy in the larger context of the strategy I'd seen Minnesota take toward the redesign of large public systems. That's this book, revised now for a second time. A kind of memoir, with the education policy story embedded in it.

Ideas come together and action comes closer

Education|Evolvng is working more itself, and now with the Bush Foundation, on student-centered-learning. That contains the concept of competency-based progression: letting students move as far and as fast as they can go. As these ideas develop some new dimensions are opening for the policy discussion.

Conspicuous cases are causing people to notice, for example, that 'competency-based' is common in athletics. Ninth-graders, eighth-graders, sometimes seventh-graders can move up to the varsity in hockey, in tennis, in basketball and other sports. In 2020 we read about Paige Bueckers, now the starting point guard for the nation's top women's university basketball team, doing things no player at the University of Connecticut has done—which is saying a lot. She was on the varsity at Hopkins when in eighth-grade. Sunisa Lee made the American senior gymnastics team at 16. She came back in the fall of 2019 with a gold medal from the world championships and, if they have the Olympics this summer, might come back with another.

The question is inescapable: Why can't young people move ahead faster also in academics? Why is the curriculum still captive to age-grading? Think what we might see were it open for young people to move ahead in math, world language or biology as they can in sports.

Questions seem inescapable, too, with respect to the system. Over the years almost every governmental institution in Minnesota has been changed, modernized. Commissions have been replaced by commissioners. New departments, like Finance, have appeared in the state administration. An intermediate court of appeals was established. In the 1960s a whole new level of metropolitan government was created for the Twin Cities region. In 1949, at the urging of the League of Municipalities, the Legislature put into law three optional forms of organization among which voters in Minnesota cities could choose; it led to a strengthening of city management and administration. Nothing has been done to change the standard plan of school district organization. The chairmanship of the board is passed from member to member; a kind of disagreeable duty. There is no political leadership. An 'optional forms' statute could be enacted for district public education, to provide a leadership office comparable to the mayor in city government. But nothing is done.

A challenge to the performance of Minnesota's system appeared in 2020 with the effort to amend the state constitution to give all children a civil right to a quality education. The initiative came from Neel Kashkari, president of the Federal Reserve Bank of Minneapolis, and Alan Page, a former justice of the state supreme court. Their proposal got lost that year due to the pandemic. It was pushed again, and harder, in 2021. But with the teachers union publicly opposed, allowing the major education associations to avoid taking a position, the Legislature at this writing seemed likely to defer a decision. The campaign, however, revealed significant dissatisfaction in the citizenry, in the business community and among people in local government. If the sense of the need for change continues to build into the '22 session, the Legislature will be hard put to refuse to send the proposed amendment to the ballot.

The problem with the Page amendment was that it offered no 'how'. Essentially it was a Brexit; a proposal that the government put to the voters an appealing and widely supported goal with no one knowing how it would be implemented, or what the consequences would be were it to be implemented (or what the political consequences would be were it not). If the initiative is to succeed it will be essential to define 'quality education' and to think out what will need to be done to create a system capable of realizing that goal. This will be a discussion in which young people will assert their claim to be full participants, arguing perhaps that 'quality education' means a system that offers every student the opportunity to realize his/her potential.

CHAPTER 22:

The Strategy for Change Comes Clear

Someone conspicuously successful in public life wrote that at their heart even complex problems are simple, but that people come to this understanding only when starting from an unexpected direction and only after working through the distractions and confusions that stand in the way.

The problem in public education was simple. It lay in the system design, which (See page 180) had the state assuring the districts their economic success whether or not they changed and improved and whether or how well the students learned. It was an institution controlled by adults, to serve adult interests; the model Horace Mann, who admired the bureaucratic arrangement in that rising north German state, brought back from Prussia in 1843. It is a model which, we can now see, is not in the students' interest, not in the public interest. It gave us a static system.

The simple truth is also that no significant redesign of school and system was possible so long as it involved and required changing existing schools. For a hundred years people advocated 'school reform' and designed 'better schools'—to little if any effect. To create a self-improving system there had to be a new sector in which it was possible to create new public schools in which innovation could be tried; then, as these innovations proved attractive, for them to move into the mainline district sector. A simple strategy.

In Minnesota since the 1960s the growing variety of 'alternative' schools and programs has begun to make that strategy operate. This was not consciously planned. It came as a set of practical responses by this state to needs and problems as they appeared. It transformed public education from a regulated public utility into an array of public choices among different forms of school and different approaches to teaching and learning.

Many of the new schools created have picked up the simple central conclusion Jack Frymier expressed: that any successful effort to improve student learning will begin by improving student motivation (See page 197). We've now begun the process of moving that process of maximizing student motivation, and the needed opportunity for teachers to change the way they work with students, into the district sector. Personalizing learning will at the same time enlarge teachers' professional role. Motivated students and motivated teachers are both good things; making public education more successful in ways that will serve the interest of the state government and of the systems itself—as well as the interest of parents and students.

This, then, is the strategy. It *is* simple, at its heart. It has just taken us a long time to get there.

So what stands in the way?

A strategy that begins with letting people try things, with R&D, succeeds only as it spreads into the mainline system. So to get to scale this strategy for improving school and learning, simple as it is, will have to be adopted in the existing district system.

There are three ways it might be implemented. One is to allow and encourage the 'alternative' sector (broadly defined) to grow and perhaps, in time, to replace the conventional district sector. That possibility was contemplated in the study of alternative "futures of school reform" organized by the Harvard Graduate School of Education, its report published in 2012. A second is for districts themselves to create new and different schools. A third is for districts to arrange for their *existing* schools to become different; boards and superintendents telling teachers and administrators they may change their approach to learning, their use of time, even their 'spaces', in order to develop more personal and more successful relationships with students.

The first two run into difficulties with districts. Districts will not want to be *replaced*. The 'utility' mentality survives in the 'traditional notion that public education *is* the district system. The resistance to 'someone else' offering public education can be heard in the charge, for example, that chartered schools are "taking *our* money". And a proposal to create a new and innovative school within the district can encounter opposition from the district's conventional schools, concerned about losing enrollment. These internal differences create conflict between schools and between parent groups. Better, boards conclude, to keep things the same, across the schools and down through time.

The third however, avoiding structural change, essentially allowing and encouraging teachers to personalize learning in their own courses and classes, is hopeful. It avoids the obstacles confronting the other two approaches. But it still must overcome the fundamental problem that comes with any challenge to the old Horace Mann model, and to adults' accustomed ways of doing things.

Allowing teachers to personalize learning is hopeful.

The notion that traditional school is 'real school' goes deep, in the institution and in the public; creating the inertia that innovation must overcome. Experienced consultants say the most difficult challenge in their work "is to overcome the client's resistance to rigorous diagnosis". Those proposing changes in education know what that means.

If you looked at the video of Mr. Pai (See page 197) you'll have heard him "stunned" by the "bureaucratic apathy" of those who were impressed but then would do nothing. He was encountering the feeling that change is unneeded and unnatural. "Fold your arms across your chest", a speaker said one year to the Minnesota School Boards Association. "OK, now cross them the other way." They did. "Doesn't feel right, does it", she said.

Just as deep is the notion that 'education' is something adults do to children; clear in the conventional language that sees education being "delivered". The curriculum is set by adults, with courses required and 'standards' adopted for students. (I once saw a document half an inch thick setting out just what every student should know about libraries.) Teachers teach what's required and it is assumed that students will learn if told they must. "We make students work more on what they do least well and like least", says one Minnesota superintendent. "Why don't we let them work more on what they do best and like most?"

The system does not treat students as co-workers on the job of learning—which they clearly are. Unpaid, they have to be compensated with opportunity. But the system is not built and operated around the idea of eliciting from them that "extra level of discretionary effort" (See page 206). Nor is a district often seriously interested in asking its students how well it is doing. So the performance of students everywhere, of all students, falls short of what they could be achieving and of what the state now needs. In Minnesota most do score well on the old-fashioned conventional assessments—which produces Minnesota's notorious 'achievement gap'. Some don't. But they graduate. Politically, the system cannot afford not to have them graduate.

The challenge, for strategy, is to find a way to spread change into and through the mainline district system, motivating young people to the higher level of accomplishment of which they are capable.

Realistically, successful change will be voluntary and gradual

We start with the fact that conventional 'strategies' have consistently failed. "School has changed reform more than reform has changed school", says Larry Cuban, long in the school of education at Stanford. Efforts at 'reform' have varied from showing an exemplary new school and hoping those seeing its virtues will adopt it, to national legislation tying mandates to federal grants. Neither approach has been notably successful; not the exemplary-model and not "No Child Left Behind" requiring states to set standards, test achievement and enforce accountability.

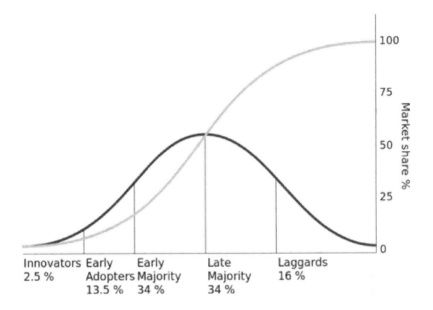

Innovators	Early	Early	Late	Laggards
2.5 %	Adopters	Majority	Majority	16 %
	13.5 %	34 %	34 %	

A successful strategy will have to be more than the former and less than the latter. It should start as an effort to develop new models of school and approaches to learning. Chartering does that, being open for schools to be as different as their organizers wish. The 'R&D' strategy does not mandate change: Districts can if they wish pick up models and approaches developed there, but they need not. Change is voluntary. And because it is voluntary it will be gradual. This follows the model Everett Rogers set out in **Diffusion of Innovations.**

This is better, actually, than trying to do everything at once. It means change starts and proceeds with those ready and willing for the radically different. The more voluntary the change, the more radical it can be: You are working with those who are ready. Change will then be gradual, but 'gradual' need not mean 'slow'. Think about how quickly innovations in the world of digital electronics have spread.

We really are making progress

This voluntary and gradual process is visible in the transformation of public education in Minnesota, from the traditional district-public-utility model to its current array of public options. Certainly this is a major change, and one that can be described as progress.

The sense of the need for change is spreading. So too is the discussion about innovation. In the national discussion this often appears as 'next-generation learning' or 'deeper learning', though one senses there is sometimes more discussion than action. Minnesota has secondary schools that have all their students doing project-based learning, and even a few online project-based schools.

Here there is growing pressure for still further change, from very different directions. From one direction, certainly the campaign for a constitutional amendment guaranteeing children a 'quality education' is an example (See pages 210–211). From another, young people have begun to organize to assert their interests in better education. Organized as People for PSEO, for example, current and former users of that 1985 program (which lets juniors and seniors finish high school in college) are now asking the Legislature to deal with the districts' reluctance to tell students about the opportunity, and administrators' tendency to put obstacles in their way. They are effective: Legislators like what they learn when they listen to students. They are organizing, too, in another field, to change the rule than has denied young people unemployment compensation because they are students.

Times have changed. Educational needs have changed. Young people have changed. Mary Lee Fitzgerald's comment comes back to mind (she having been a superintendent in New Jersey and later state commissioner of education): "Our high schools used to be filled with children. Today they're filled with young people who are essentially adults—being treated still as children."

The national discussion lags; dominated still by the political commitment 20 years ago to the accountability model: standards, testing and consequences; a "one-bet strategy" as the chair of the California state board put it to me once, that has not worked out well.

A 'one-bet' strategy is a risk. It is not a necessary risk: We could be trying other approaches—could for example, be working to maximize student engagement—at the same time. Perhaps Minnesota is itself a kind of split-screen strategy; going its own way, using the R&D model, the Everett Rogers model, operating at the level of the nation as a whole its; innovations being copied by other states as these decide they are ready. Chartering certainly seems an example, 'diffusing' to about 40 states in about a decade.

It is a process of change that can apply in other areas of public life as well. Let's consider that, in closing.

SECTION SEVEN:

THE 'NEW NATIONALISM' RUNS TO ITS END

One major conclusion has been developing for me as I have been revising this book. Put simply: It is time now to move on from the concept Herbert Croly sold to Theodore Roosevelt in 1910: 'The New Nationalism', the idea of moving decisions into the public sector, up to the national level and over to the executive branch.

Today the national government is overloaded; its politics and its decision-making capability overwhelmed by its responsibilities. It is all the Congress and the Presidency can do to handle foreign affairs, defense, homeland security and the economy. Washington is overwhelmed by its truly national responsibilities: national defense; foreign policy, coping with the astonishing rise of China; homeland security and immigration; the management of the economy.

Recent developments are calling into question both the advisability of nationalizing decisions and of letting them become so largely decisions for the national executive.

Section Five set out a significantly different concept of 'the public sector'. Problems in the 'life-support systems' of the urban regions in which three-quarters of Americans now live—transportation, public safety, housing, energy, education, environmental protection—are in a sense nationwide. From there it's an easy step to thinking that anything nationwide is 'a national problem' and to assume that 'a national problem' must be handled by the national government.

Those in the national government are almost irresistibly tempted to get involved in domestic problems. Yet experience has shown it is better not to try to run domestic systems from the center. The effort at 'national urban policy' through regional councils of governments failed. After 30 years of effort the core problems in public education remain. Nor has Washington been able to deal with cost and quality in the medical-hospital system.

The standard tools available to the national government—regulations, and grants with regulations attached—can start things, and can block things, but they do not do well handling change, especially where the need is to improve effectiveness and efficiency; to *redesign* public systems that operate under state rather than national law.

Redesign challenges the 'givens' of a system . . . and changing the existing arrangements is something those running any system are always loath to do: At either the state or national level, they prefer change *within* the givens. Successful efforts at redesign emerge, however, not from the 'stakeholders' but from those whose careers are *not* at stake. That requires a civic sector; institutions and individuals able to raise an issue, define a problem, shape a proposal and influence the decision—accepted or implemented by the public bodies that carry the responsibility for the problem in question.

National politics and policymaking is a contest among interest groups, in which a viable civic sector is seldom seen. Only in the states and at the local level is there some possibility of finding institutions and individuals capable of performing this civic function.

That civic process is what this book has been about . . . and at the end, as we consider how it can be revived and restored in the light of our current situation, it will be useful to recap its essential concepts.

CHAPTER 23:

Our Democracy Has a Local Foundation

In his seminar on state and local government at Princeton's school of public affairs John Sly started with the Colonial period. That made sense, because it was obvious that in those days communication was captive to transportation, and with England weeks away by ship, King George's ability to command and control was limited. That made it natural for local institutions to appear—aided perhaps by the congregational traditions of the early immigrants from East Anglia.

Through the years this decentralization persisted,, and became a valued feature of American democracy. Among other things, our states and communities provided the training for policymaking. De Tocqueville in 1832 wrote: *"The greater the multiplicity of small affairs, the more do men, even without knowing it, acquire facility in prosecuting great undertakings in common."*

Minnesota's own members of Congress—Bill Frenzel and Martin Sabo in particular—were notably skeptical about the superiority of Washington wisdom—impressed, as I once heard Sabo say, by "our ability out here in Washington to screw things up". One useful response was to pull the states together into a national organization. Sabo helped found the National Conference of State Legislatures. Wanting some national—but not national government—policy for public education, James B. Conant proposed, and saw the creation of, the Education Commission of the States. Jack Davies, as a Minnesota state senator, worked with the Commission on Uniform State Laws.

Some questions do require national decision; legislation or executive action, or a judgment by the Supreme Court. The desegregation of southern schools surely an example. But some 'national' solutions do emerge from legislation beginning in a single state and spreading across the states; as, between 1910 and 1920 and encouraged by the U.S. Department of Labor, workers compensation. Compulsory education is another. The appearance and spread of chartering after 1991 fits this pattern. "Laboratories of democracy", is the term Justice Brandeis applied to the process.

Against this, though, the pressure for centralization has been remorseless. Paul Ylvisaker, a Minnesotan, noted the general tendency of 'higher' levels of government to take power away from 'lower'. After 1950 Congress began preempting various policy areas, asserting its jurisdiction. Grants-in-aid to the states increasingly had strings attached. The tendency was reinforced by single-interest groups, as organized campaigns from women's suffrage to prohibition went to Congress for legislation (or for a constitutional amendment) hoping to achieve their goal at a single stroke.

Gradually too, as the telegraph, telephone, radio, television and now the internet have liberated communication from transportation, information can be exchanged almost instantaneously, enlarging greatly the ability for central command and control.

More and more too, it seems, the media points to the executive as the person to 'take charge'; personifying the president: What *should* 'he' do? What *will* 'he' do? Presidents of both parties are displaying willingness to bypass the legislative process and act by executive order: Bush and Obama, Trump and Biden.

We do not yet have quite what the British refer to as their "elective dictatorship", but it is not unreasonable to feel that the idea Herbert

Croly sold to Theodore Roosevelt in 1910 as an expansion of democracy—'into the public sector, up to the national level, over to the
executive branch' ... the idea of 'the executive as the steward of the
public welfare'—has passed its time; is not the right prescription for our
time. President Biden's assertion that the president is the voice of our
democracy, especially when combined with the powers conferred by
The Patriot Act enacted following 9/11, is worrisome.

The civic role in the policy process

A good place to start as we go back to the civic process is with the
graphic you saw earlier (page 160). A short 'refresher' might be in order.

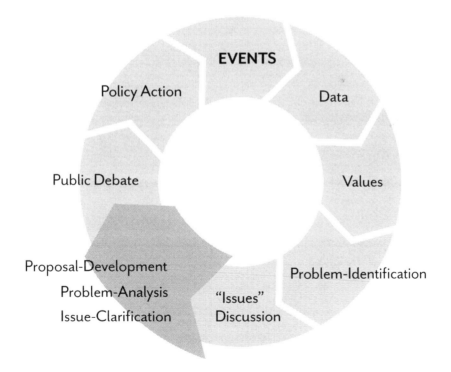

Start at the top with Events; things happening. A railroad tank
car overturns and explodes, for example. This ('data') is quickly and
widely seen, now that the surveillance camera and cellphone video are

everywhere. As events intersect with values a problem is identified. A discussion begins. Everyone deplores the problem; everyone wants this not to happen again. Which takes the process to the critical point. Those sure they know whom to hold responsible want to jump immediately to 'policy action'. But others are inclined to ask, "Why do these accidents happen?" and to say, "If we found the causes, maybe we could keep it from happening again." That starts a process of analysis, of learning enough to develop a proposal to solve the underlying problem.

You can run most public problems around this cycle. Clarifying the issue, understanding the causes of things, developing proposals for actions that get down to causes—this is what proves effective. But it is hard for the organizations directly involved, because it often requires some major change in their system. And the media are impatient: reporting the 'why' and the 'how' was never the nature of television. And the newspapers now say "We don't do 'process' stories".

Consider the discussion since George Floyd died under a police-man's knee. Values were asserted, problems identified. The criminal trial assessed the officer's responsibility. But quite different views remain about 'the police', and no clarity has yet emerged about how to get a chief of police to deal with 'thumpers' on the force. An early answer from the City Council to de-fund the police was not persuasive with neighborhoods that need police protection. Perhaps something useful will come from the Charter Commission. Minneapolis still awaits the needed thinking-out.

This is the role for the civic sector; the individuals and organizations willing and able to take the time and make the effort required to under-stand the 'why' of problems.

Minnesota has been good at this, as I hope readers of this book will agree: the business community, the newspapers, the groups that gather around breakfast, lunch and dinner tables to talk about public questions.

At the same time—as I hope readers will also have seen—this civic sector has deteriorated. Some business firms now find Washington more important than the state capital; others have simply left public affairs.

The newspapers no longer have people covering the public debate about policy action. The city magazines cover private life, not public, life. The foundations are cautious.

Yet work does continue on the questions of system redesign.

As the 2008 fiscal crisis and the squeeze on state finances created a sense of a 'new normal', former Governor Arne Carlson put perfectly the 'how' question for state leadership: We can't just cut our way out; we can't just tax our way out; we can't count on growing our way out, he said. We have to think our way out. That put redesign on Minnesota's public agenda.

We have to think our way out.

Dan Loritz and Curt Johnson got me on the agenda for the annual meeting of what is now the Minnesota Center for Fiscal Excellence. In a talk I titled "We Can Change the Way We Do Things" I tried to get people thinking about changing the mechanism inside the box that turns resources into results.

The three of us went to foundations to recall the work done on redesign during the '70s and '80s. Carleen Rhodes at the Saint Paul Foundation and Sandra Vargas at the Minneapolis Foundation responded. Several foundations got together in a contract with Public Strategies to come up with major redesign initiatives: 'Minnesota's Bottom Line'.

Dan and Walter McClure changed the Center for Policy Studies to the Center for Policy Design. It worked up several case studies explaining important redesigns: ridesharing, assisted living, hospital reorganization. Later I pulled together a broader set of documents about redesign from PSO onward, showing how much had resulted. Dan put together a Redesign Discussion Group; people from organizations across the policy spectrum that met for dinner at Muffuletta monthly for four years.

The state associations of counties and of cities began thinking about redesign. In the Legislature an informal 'redesign caucus'—led by Representatives Paul Marquart, DFL, and Carol McFarlane, Republican—formed and held hearings.

Verne Johnson, until his death, was chairing the CIVIC Caucus; its weekly interviews of persons in public policy in and outside government combining the old Citizens League breakfasts and committee sessions.

Its important effort at the need for redesign—and at the region's capacity to generate 'settings' for that work—continued as CIVIC transitioned into new leadership.

Can innovation combine equity and effectiveness?

The recession, and the slowness of the recovery from it, reminded the country of some economic realities: about the way digital technology is disrupting industry after industry, raising concerns about jobs and careers, about the growing need for a broadened concept of social responsibility, and about the need for priorities in a time of constrained finances.

As a region and as a nation we are likely to be challenged by the need to reconcile the aspirations for social and personal 'fulfillment' with the reality of an economy growing more slowly than in the past. Daniel Yankelovich described in **New Rules** in 1981 the shift in the 1960s from the old 'ethic of self-denial' to the new 'ethic of self-fulfillment'— for individuals and for society. That seemed possible then: John Borchert had described 1950-1975 as "The quarter-century of greatest increase in real output the world has ever known". Affluence seemed the norm.

Not so, now; as Yankelovich himself advised. It is that quarter-century of affluence that looks now to be exceptional. The norm is likely to be economic growth of more like two per cent per year, as Marc Levinson writes in **An Extraordinary Time**. Simultaneously, we are experiencing extraordinary economic, social and technological change that creates new demands for social responsibility.

The challenge will be to accommodate these conflicting forces. The tendency—evident in a series of forums at the Humphrey School—has been to set out the needs for pensions, for transportation, for infrastructure, for housing, for child care; each concluding, as I recall: This will be expensive, but this is a rich country; we can afford it. I do not recall a program putting all these needs together ... responding with policies and programs that are simultaneously effective and economical.

To put the central conclusion simply: Just as in public education the success of the district sector depends on there being a successful charter sector, so in our public affairs broadly the success of the political sector depends on there being a successful civic sector.

Successful politics requires a strong civic sector

Early in 2016 I picked up the project I'd started a few years before; this book, aiming to describe and explain the public affairs I've watched since I started here 60 years ago. As I say in the preface, this has taken me back to broader questions about the public sector that set the larger frame into which my recent work on education fits. I have been considering what this civic activity might look like in the years ahead.

The civic role that seems essential is a challenging role. Institutions do not appreciate being pushed. Their people appeal for 'collaboration': Don't fight us; work with us—which of course means accepting the pace at which those inside are willing to change. But those outside, in the civic sector, need to push . . . tactfully, making clear they are attacking not the people inside, but the system in which those people work. That pressure from the outside will help, and will be appreciated by those inside who *are* working for change and whose voice would otherwise be suppressed or ignored.

I now see the civic role having three elements:

- **Scanning**, to identify early the problems and opportunities coming over the horizon.

- **Thinking; designing.** Organizing settings in which people who understand the system in which these coming-developments occur can think about what in its structure is causing the problem and what redesign of the system-architecture might correct the problem.

- **Acting.** Getting proposals moved onto the agendas of the individuals and organizations able to make change in our public systems and institutions.

Let's take them in order.

- **The scanning.** This shouldn't be difficult: Specialists in most fields have a sense for changes in the offing and for the adjustments needed. Somebody will have to collect these perceptions. The challenge will be to select those that should go out for study. Decisions will turn on who else will be thinking about them and perhaps on which are actionable at the state level. An example of what someone ought to be picking up right now is what's clearly 'on the horizon' with changes in the automobile. More and more of us might soon be using an app to summon a battery-powered vehicle that we do not have to own that will take us quickly and at reasonable cost directly to our destination without our having to drive it. The auto industry is realistic; seems to have accepted this radically new future as inevitable. In September 2016 the New York Times wrote: "*The Chevy Bolt (electric vehicle) is not only the first inexpensive long-range electric car on the road; it will also function as GM's platform for testing new models for ride-sharing and autonomous driving.*"

    The growing sense of transportation as a service has potential to develop a whole new concept of urban mobility in the Twin Cities area. It might be disruptive for public works, for parking and for auto insurance. But it might produce quality improvements (fewer accidents/injuries) and efficiency gains (reduced capital expenditures on autos, roads and garages and in expenditures for gasoline, parking and insurance). Certainly it will prompt a re-thinking about 'transit'; a much-needed reappraisal in the Twin Cities area of the counties' push to spend billions on a rail system that cannot get very many people from home to where they want to go. The change in mobility is likely to come faster than the policy discussion can adapt: The old conception of transit dies hard. On my wall hangs an ad from a major national corporation promoting "efficient mass transportation" and urging the country to "get on with it". The message is illustrated with a rocket ship from a 1939 Flash Gordon comic strip.

Perhaps some day someone will see the need to do something about the institution of 'adolescence' that discriminates so powerfully against our youth.

- **Analyzing**. The next step will be to get the top-priority questions into one of the 'settings' (see Chapter 16) to be thought-about: individuals or organizations, existing organizations or new. The need to think in terms of changing system-structure will challenge the conventional impulse that favors incremental change, but hold tight to the importance of getting at causes; resist the pressure to compromise proposals. It will be a learning process for all involved.

  Some financing will be needed, but as Chapter 19 reports about Education|Evolving, not necessarily a lot. Happily, experienced people are likely to be available as volunteers. Out of the settings will come the analysis and the proposals for actions to be taken.

  The dreadful discussion about 'health care' in early 2017 showed the need for a fundamental rethinking. It was largely about the politics of financing care, and dealt hardly at all with the problems in the medical/hospital system itself; the perverse incentives that drive costs and the problems of quality that are largely concealed from public view. (It is only now coming to light that medical error is a major cause of mortality and morbidity.) The policy discussion needs to address these problems; needs to talk about solutions that, as Walter McClure says, involve "identifying the high-quality, low-cost clinics and hospitals and arranging the benefit programs to flow them patients". It is a redesign that will have to come, he says, one metropolitan area at a time.

- **Acting**. Once developed in the civic sector, proposals for change can be taken to those in political life to use for their own and the public's benefit. The political system needs, depends on those outside for bold proposals. The point is made perfectly in Monnet's **Memoirs:** *"Governments always find it difficult, and very often impossible, to change the existing state of affairs which it is their duty to administer . . . They have to account to Parliament, and they are held back by their officials, who want to keep everything just so . . . Change can come only from the outside, under the pressure of necessity . . . (Those in office) do not always have either the taste or the time for using their imagination. They are open to creative ideas, and anyone who knows to present such ideas has a good chance of having them accepted."*

And a strong civic sector requires successful politics

To the extent it will be necessary to move analyses and proposals directly to people in policy roles, one useful adaptation would be to redesign the electoral system to improve the chances of bringing into office persons more receptive to system change, more inclined to get to the causes of problems.

Tony Solgard, in private life a Minnesotan running a bookkeeping service, came back from a visit to Scandinavia in 1996 talking about the different voting systems there. America, he noted, had recently had various elections in which more than two candidates were offering programs; new political ideas were appearing. But the third candidate arguing for 'different' usually lost; often splitting the vote with the result that a candidate identified with one polar position or the other was elected with a minority of the vote.

The appearance of ranked-choice voting (RCV) offers another approach . . . that might help speed policy change. This system—earlier known as 'instant runoff voting'—makes it possible for citizens to support a candidate offering new ideas without 'wasting your vote' and makes it possible for a candidate to advance a new approach without being criticized as a spoiler for 'splitting the vote'.

Solgard's discussions led to a League of Women Voters study of alternate systems, which about 2005 produced a recommendation for ranked-choice voting. The new system was introduced in Minneapolis; later worked to elect a mayor. It was adopted in Saint Paul in 2009. Fair-Vote Minnesota was formed to help other local jurisdictions interested in ranked-choice voting.

Conventional politicians fight it; the established parties dislike it—with reason. In September 2017 Michael Porter at Harvard Business School and Katherine Gehl, a business-person turned reformer in Wisconsin, looked at politics and voting "through the lens of industry competition. They saw, and described, the two major parties as private organizations that have managed to suppress competition from third parties and from independent candidates. This perspective seems to have been muted now by the RCV campaign—which exists today, however, as an outstanding example of scanning for a problem, doing an analysis, and moving a proposal into action. Fair Vote Minnesota, Jeanne Massey its executive director, is its 'setting'.

Prospects

I hope the central conclusion is clear: That it is time for a new politics that balances social responsibility with economic responsibility . . . and that this can best be done—probably done only—at levels where the contribution from the civic sector can be effective; in the states and metropolitan communities. And that for its own success the governmental/political sector needs a successful civic sector continually pushing officials to do the things those in politics find hardest to do on their own.

Minnesota has been a successful state. When in 2003 Jack Frymier published his **Rankings of the States**—233 pages of lists showing best to worst on 701 different measures—Minnesota came through clearly as the best state in America. Its contribution to national public life has been substantial: two vice presidents and nominees for the presidency; members of the cabinet and of the Supreme Court; outstanding members of Congress. It has done well in opening to groups earlier excluded from equal status in community life. It has welcomed immigrants from Asia and Africa. Its organizations have become more diverse racially and ethnically. It was leading in programs for special education and for medical assistance before the national government acted. The attitude I heard a leading lawyer express in the 1950s, that "the women don't count", is long gone and Minneapolis is long over its anti-Semitism. It might become a leader now in getting police behavior under control.

This can continue in Minnesota if someone here will ensure we have the 'settings' necessary for this work ... arranging for younger people to have the time and resources and freedom to think, in today's quite different social context, about the causes of problems and the actions that will be effective by way of redesign.

This state and this community ... like states and communities everywhere ... are different now than in the decades I write about. A new generation has appeared, accustomed to a new technology of communication. Huge changes have appeared as social values, social attitudes, have changed; law and policy reacting and adapting in response. Policymaking is different; decisions made less in formal institutions and more by protests and pressures. Many social decisions are made not politically but by changes in public attitudes and behaviors and by technological innovations disrupting existing institutions, private and public.

Still, much of our success, our 'quality of life', is *made* here, by what we do in our public life. With our comparative advantage in institutional adaptation Minnesota could show the way; could be the first state to realign the ideas of its public life, and to develop a process of electoral politics that speeds the transition.

Maintaining our advantage in institutional adaptation is essential to assure Minnesota's own future. It would be nice if, in addition, we could be the state that turned around the nation's political discussion.

As existing institutions continue to be pressed to adapt, the question will remain: How to make those adjustment most quickly, most smoothly and most appropriately. The most successful states and cities will be those able to develop and maintain a superior capacity for thinking out the 'how'.

ABOUT THE AUTHOR

Ted Kolderie is a co-founder (along with Joe Graba) of Education|Evolving. He and his wife, Marjorie, live in Saint Paul.

He can be reached at ted@educationevolving.org. More is available about this 'design shop', its people and its policy proposals at www.educationevolving.org.

He is a senior fellow also at the Center for Policy Design, where various of his publications can be read and downloaded at www.centerforpolicy.org.

CENTER FOR POLICY DESIGN PRESS

Mission

The mission of the Center for Policy Design Press (CPD Press) is to advance the field of large system analysis and redesign through publishing selected high-quality work on the theory and practice, and serve as a resource center through development of educational and curricular content for students, researchers, policy makers and other concerned citizens.

CPD Press publications reflect CPD core values, including:
- The centrality of system thinking for successful policy design.
- Verifiability of facts and truth.
- The power of creative thinking.
- Non-partisanship.
- Civility.
- Inclusion of multiple perspectives.
- More effective education of today's and tomorrow's policy design leaders

Vision

The CPD Press vision is to be a resource leader in publishing impactful materials that advance design of sound policy for large systems. Press publications will, collectively, be widely recognized for offering creative thinking, rigorous research, sound analysis, and promise of utility in policy design and policy implementation.

CPD Press publishes written materials of various types and lengths, including: Books, Reports, Working papers, Memos and Op-Eds, and External publications (e.g. previously published works, by special arrangement.)

Unsolicited manuscripts are not accepted.

Made in the USA
Monee, IL
13 June 2022

97944586R00138